JESUS

AUTHOR & FINISHER

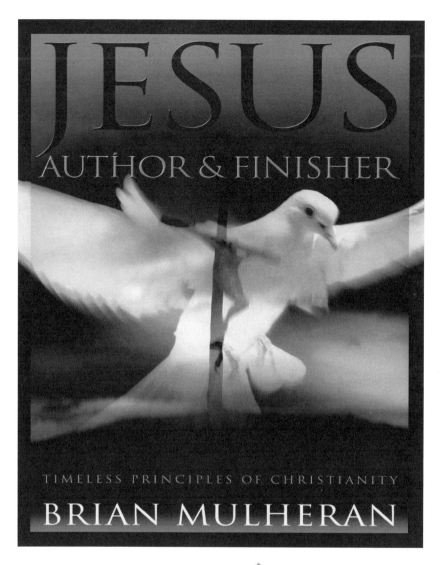

JESUS
AUTHOR & FINISHER

TIMELESS PRINCIPLES OF CHRISTIANITY

BRIAN MULHERAN

SYNERGY Publishers
Gainesville, Florida 32614 USA

A division of Bridge-Logos International Trust
in partnership with **Bridge-Logos** *Publishers*

Jesus, Author & Finisher
by Brian Mulheran
© 2002 by Brian Mulheran. All rights reserved

International Standard Book Number: 1-931727-05-8
Library of Congress Catalog Card Number: 2001098428

Published by:
Synergy Publishers
Gainesville, Florida 32614 USA
www.synergypublishers.com

Synergy Publishers is a division of Bridge-Logos International Trust, Inc., in partnership with Bridge-Logos Publishers.

DEDICATION

To Viv, Benjamin, Kate and Matthew

You are my inspiration and my world!

CONTENTS

FOREWORD

If the foundations are destroyed,
what can the righteous do?—Psalm 11:3

The Bible teaches us the need for laying solid foundations. When we understand truths, we can walk in the might and freedom those truths bring into our lives. One such truth that has impacted City Harvest Church is the understanding that we need to renew our minds all the time.

Do You Want to Lead or Crouch in Fear?

When God placed Adam and Eve in the Garden of Eden, He gave them dominion over all His creation on the earth (Genesis 1:26–28). Although Adam was limited in physical strength, he had the divine authority to rule over the beasts of the field, many of which were much bigger and stronger than he was. However, Adam had the ability to strategize and outmaneuver the lions and tigers.

When Adam sinned against God, none of the animals changed in their size and might. But one thing did change in Adam—his mind became darkened. When that happened, he lost the ability to rule and to lead. Instead, he became fearful of the elements around him. From that moment, this has become the legacy of all human beings.

The Twelve Foundations of Faith

We are all born with the Adamic nature and with Adam's many weaknesses. However, by the power of the Holy Spirit, we can change all that. We can renew our minds daily and be transformed into the likeness of the unlimited Christ.

Jesus Author and Finisher, written by Brian Mulheran, can give you the necessary understanding to renew your mind. As you pour through the pages, let God speak to your heart. And as your understanding increases, your life will take on a whole new dimension in God. You'll start taking dominion over every challenge in your life.

Kong Hee
City Harvest Church
Singapore

ACKNOWLEDGMENTS

Nothing worth doing in life is ever done alone. It is with all my heart that I treasure the special people in my life who have joined with me in producing this work.

Thanks to my wife Viv, my princess, my inspiration, my companion and best friend—you have been my lifeline, my constant support and my greatest encourager. You always bring out the best in me and cause me to go further than I would ever have dreamed. To our three precious children—Benjamin, Kate and Matthew—you are our world and you brighten up every one of our days. I am so proud to be your dad. I want to honor you before all the people who read and study this book; you have invested your time into every one of their lives.

Thanks to my family, especially you, Mum. You're my number one fan. Your prayers and encouragement are beyond words. I am forever indebted to you for your love and bringing me to the place of believing in Jesus. You have continually shaped my life in God and brought me up in His ways. Thanks Dad for establishing godly principles in my life and shaping my standards. Your have instilled values into me that have kept me throughout the years. Thanks to my four brothers Steve, Mike, Pete and Chris for helping to shape my life in more ways than one. You guys are the best. You are my closest friends. Thanks for always being there to talk and share with me. Thanks for the times you have stayed up late and listened to my latest revelations without falling asleep. Thanks also to their wonderful wives: Julie, Nadine, Leonie and Donagh and my precious nephews and nieces for giving me the honor of experiencing true community.

Thanks to my "fathers and mothers" in the faith whose constant belief in me has caused me to pursue my destiny. Your vision, your faith and your words of inspiration and encouragement continue to shape my life. To Neil and Nance

Miers and David and Tricia McDonald: I could search the world ten times over and still not find the caliber of people who could speak into my life as you have. "Thank you" just doesn't seem to do justice.

Thanks to my personal assistant, Jill Lloyd and husband Darren, for your tireless work of typing, proofreading and research. Thanks for your inspiration and keeping me accountable with your e-mails. (One of Jill's first e-mails stated, "I'm going to be the PA of a very famous author one day. Are you helping me to achieve my goals?")

Thanks to Dennis Watson, Marianne Graves and the team at Synergy for your belief, support, encouragement and spirit of excellence.

Thanks to Paul and Maureen Cant for your assistance and advice. It has been invaluable. Without you I don't know if this book would have reached first base.

Thanks to Don and Heather Stieler for your belief in us and your support when we needed it most. Thanks to Mary Hawken who is the modern day version of the widow with her two mites.

Special thanks to Reverend Kong Hee and Dr. Phil Pringle for your time and encouragement in reviewing the book amid your busy schedules.

Thanks to Mark and Leigh Ramsey and my friends and staff of Citipointe Christian Outreach Centre, Brisbane and our incredible congregation. You are all truly inspirational; I couldn't wish to be part of a better team or a greater church.

Thanks to the staff and students of Citipointe International Institute of Ministry. You have allowed me to speak the truths in this book into your lives and equip you as spirit-filled leaders who are "Destined to make a Difference."

Finally, thanks to the Christians I have gleaned from over the years. It is likely you could see some of your thoughts in various forms throughout the book. A special thanks to Mike Williams for some of his teaching. A number of points within the book have been inspired by his original thoughts.

INTRODUCTION

A great cloud of witnesses surrounds us. Filling the heavenly grandstand these heroes of faith rise as one to inspire us to the finish. They stand victorious as those who have already run the race and fought the good fight. As spectators who have persevered and endured, triumphed and conquered, they now cheer for us. Their acclamation sounds through the commentary of the apostle to "lay aside every weight and sin ... and run the race looking to Jesus the author and finisher of our faith" (Hebrews 12:1–2).

Look to the stands and behold the lives that Jesus has already authored and finished. Behold their accomplishments and their splendor. They have already been where we now stand. They have already struggled where we now struggle. And yet they beckon us on to the same victory they achieved through Jesus. Their cry of encouragement is that none would falter or quit and that those who are continuing would rise to greater heights. Let their cry echo through your being until every part of you is focused on Jesus the author and finisher of your faith.

Any ordinary person can ...
- let the negatives of life keep him down
- follow scriptural "dos and don'ts" to appear right with God
- try to keep himself in God to make it to heaven
- pray and read the Bible enough to look godly.

The Bible is full of extraordinary truths for ordinary people like you and me. Let's allow our extraordinary God to do extraordinary things through us as He did through the heroes of faith.

What could God do through a person who …

- focused on fulfilling God's call, instead of whether or not he sinned?
- knew she was totally righteous and could stand before God at all times?
- knew that God could not fail to do anything He said?
- knew that God wouldn't receive an accusation against a justified person?
- knew that nothing formed against him would prosper?
- knew that she had the unlimited resources of heaven at her disposal?
- knew that God was totally for him?
- knew that she possessed everything that pertained to life and godliness?

As you read the material addressed in this book, you'll discover like the heroes of faith that you are that person! It is my heart's desire that, through this discovery, you would …

- know your extraordinary God and the extraordinary things He has done
- be secure enough to trust Him to do extraordinary things through you
- look to Jesus, the author and finisher of your faith, and lay a strong foundation
- fulfill the call that God has placed upon your life
- establish firmly in your life the twelve foundations of faith I've outlined.

Whether you are a new Christian, an older Christian, or a pastor or leader desiring to establish people in the faith—this book will help you to establish firm foundations from which to build your lives. Each chapter is equipped with key points, scriptures and a study guide to assist you in building these truths deep within.

Don't treat this book as one simply to be read—write notes in the margins, highlight key points, write an action plan—deface the book until it looks like you have written it yourself. Then you will have gone a long way to writing it into your heart.

CHAPTER 1

JESUS, OUR FIRM FOUNDATION

On September 21, 1999, at exactly 1:47 A.M., a massive earthquake hit the island of Taiwan, killing 2,413 people. Families who were peacefully asleep in their beds found themselves plummeting to a final resting place of those who had previously occupied the fourth floor. Screams of horror filled the night air as foundations gave way and sent the buildings crumbling.

It was the worst quake since 1935, which reached a similar magnitude of 7.4 on the Richter scale and killed 3,276 people. Sixty-four years of minor quakes and a building boom had lulled building contractors into substandard construction. Buildings that should have been designed to withstand the quake, gave way. The people demanded that the government take action against those responsible in the building industry.

According to one CNN report, "Many of the building collapses were blamed on the unscrupulous contractors who ignored building codes or skimped on materials. Some builders mixed cans and newspapers in the concrete ... while others saved money by cutting back on reinforcement rods in the foundations."[1]

1

Our Foundation

The Apostle Paul said, "According to the grace of God which was given to me, as a wise master builder I have laid the foundation, and another builds upon it. But let each one take heed how he builds on it. For no other foundation can anyone lay than that which is laid, which is Jesus Christ" (1 Corinthians 3:10–11).

The foundation is by far the most important aspect of building our lives as Christians. If the foundation is secure, the building can be built strong and secure. If the foundation is weak or insecure, anything and everything we build upon it will be unsure and unstable.

Jesus warns us with an example of natural elements, similar to the Taiwan earthquake, which come to test the foundation of our lives. If our "house" is built on the rock, it continues to stand. If it is built on the sand, it will surely fall.

A Rock-Solid Foundation

The Apostle Paul said "no other foundation can anyone lay than that which is laid, which is Jesus Christ." Jesus is the only foundation that a Christian can have. Jesus is sure and steadfast. Many Christians fail to establish a firm foundation because they have mixed some other "substance" together with Jesus:

- Jesus and their "works"
- Jesus and their "feelings"
- Jesus and their "repentance of sin"
- Jesus and their _____

Although important fruits of faith in a Christian's life, these substances must not be mixed in the foundation. The only substance that is needed and must be in the foundation is Jesus Himself. The other substances form part of the structure we build on the foundation.

Let's have a look at why these other substances must not be added to Jesus as the foundation for our faith.

Faulty Foundations—Exposed

Works

After a series of meetings had finished, evangelist Billy Sunday was helping the workmen take down the tent. A young man who had been in the meeting the night before came up to Mr. Sunday and asked him earnestly, "What must I do to be saved?"

Sunday said, "You're too late," and kept on working.

"Don't say that," exclaimed the young man, "for I desire salvation; I would do anything or go anywhere to obtain it."

"I can't help it," Sunday replied. "You're too late; for your salvation was completed many years ago by Jesus Christ, and it's a finished work. All you can do is simply accept it. You have done nothing and can do nothing to merit salvation. It is free to all who will receive it."

When a person does something himself, this is what the Bible calls "works." Works in themselves are not wrong, except when they are "works of the flesh" or "works according to the Law." However, salvation is not by any of our works (Ephesians 2:8a).

Sometimes people are asked inadvertently to do works in order to be saved. For example, they are asked to "make Jesus Lord of their life," instead of simply, "believe on the Lord Jesus Christ" (Acts 16:31). These statements may seem very similar, but the focus can be completely the reverse if wrongly interpreted. "Believe on the Lord Jesus Christ" points to what Jesus has done in order for you to be saved. "Make Jesus Lord of your life" can, in certain ways, point you to doing something (works) for Him in order to be saved.

This last statement can (at the point of an invitation) make some question, "How many parts of my life do I need to submit to the Lordship of Jesus in order to be a "believer?" Or "What do I have to do to make Him Lord?" By thinking along these lines we place the onus for our salvation on how effectively we can "make" Jesus Lord in order to "truly believe" in Him. No person

3

throughout history has ever been able to do this completely. Many have tried and been so discouraged they gave up and fell away.

Many do not have a problem with responding properly to the call of "making Jesus Lord of their life" as it is correctly intended. I write this section to those who have misinterpreted this statement and have slipped into a works mentality.

People simply need to believe on Jesus and Him alone as the foundation. The key is putting their confidence in His finished work and not their own. From this standpoint each one can work from a position of faith, not to a position of faith.

When we put our trust in Jesus and believe in Him, He then makes us part of the Great Commission. After the disciples responded to Jesus' call, He said to them, "I will *make you* fishers of men" (Matthew 4:19 emphasis added). At Paul's conversion Jesus said, "I have appeared to you for this purpose, to *make you* a minister and a witness …" (Acts 26:16 emphasis added).

When our foundation rests solely on Jesus and we believe and put our trust in Him, He makes us complete. The writer of Hebrews sums it all up by saying, "Now may the God of peace who brought up our Lord Jesus from the dead, that great Shepherd of the sheep through the blood of the everlasting covenant, *make you complete in every good work* to do His will, *working in you* what is well pleasing in His sight, *through Jesus Christ*, to whom be glory forever and ever. Amen" (Hebrews 13:20–21 emphasis added).

Feelings

As mentioned in the previous section, sometimes the terminology used in leading people to faith in Jesus can be misleading. Terms like "invite Jesus into your heart" can cause people to question the validity of being born again if they don't feel that Jesus is on the inside any more. Many new Christians have shared with me that this has happened to them at one stage or another.

These new Christians wake up one morning and don't feel or sense Jesus on the inside as they did before and they begin to question, "Am I still born again?" At this stage, doubt enters and they wonder whether anything really happened to them because they no longer have that "wonderful feeling."

These people are basing the security of their salvation on the feeling or experience of whether Jesus still seems to be "inside them" or not.

Experiences and feelings will come and go, but God declares, "I will never leave you nor forsake you" (Hebrews 13:5). Our faith must rest solely on Jesus and Him alone, not on feelings of whether we think He is there or not. We can never totally trust our feelings, but we can totally trust Jesus. Our feelings will cause us to doubt; our faith in Jesus will cause us to stand firm.

Repentance of Sin

The term "repentance of sin" in Christianity today predominantly means to "turn away from doing what is wrong and commence doing what is right." There is no doubt that this definition is very much a positive statement for what should transpire in a person's life. However, even if you could completely turn away from doing all evil and move toward doing all that is good, would that save you? No! It is turning to belief in Jesus and what He has done for you through His sacrificial death that saves you.

When I mentioned that "repentance of sin" should not be mixed with Jesus in the foundation, I certainly didn't mean that repentance in its true sense is not part of the salvation process. But "repentance of sin" as we use the term today causes some people to doubt the steadfastness of their salvation in Jesus. They begin to wonder if they have "repented of enough sins" in order to be saved.

Charles Spurgeon wrote, "Do not regard your repentance as the cause of your remission, but as the companion of it. Do not expect to be able to repent until you are able to see the grace of

5

our Lord Jesus and His readiness to blot out your sin. Keep these blessed things in their places, and view them in their relation to each other."[2]

As Christians and Christian leaders we have often correctly said that people can come to Jesus just as they are. But somehow (and I'm sure completely unintentionally) we have often focused new converts toward "repentance of sin," as we use the term today, without clearly indicating that this should be the result, not the cause of salvation. Some people take this the wrong way and then look back to the day they believed and start to question, "Did I repent of enough sins in order to be saved?"

According to Strong's concordance, the word "repent" means to "think differently or afterwards, i.e. reconsider (morally feel compunction)."[3]

John the Baptist was the forerunner who went to prepare the way of the Lord. The question arises, "Why did Jesus need someone to go before Him and prepare the people?" The children of Israel needed to change their thinking from the Old Covenant to the New Covenant. After John the Baptist was placed in prison Jesus began preaching the gospel in Galilee saying, "The time is fulfilled, and the kingdom of God is at hand. Repent, and believe in the gospel" (Mark 1:15).

Jesus was preaching "Change your thinking and believe in the good news of My salvation which brings the remission of sins." Jesus wanted to change the Jews' thinking from trying to fulfil the Law for righteousness to believing on Him for righteousness.

It is amazing to note that in the Gospel of John, the apostle never once mentioned the word "repent" or any of its derivatives. John declares the whole purpose of his Gospel in John 20:30–31:

> And truly Jesus did many other signs in the presence of His disciples; which are not written in this book; but these are written that you may believe that Jesus is the Christ, the Son of God, and that believing you may have life in His name.

If "repentance of sins" as we use the term today caused salvation, then the Apostle John left out one of the major aspects of the gospel. However, the Gospel of John is filled from start to finish with instruction concerning eternal life in Jesus.

John 1:12 states, "But as many as received Him, to them He gave the right to become children of God, even to those who *believe* in His name." John 3:16, arguably the most quoted verse of the Bible, says "that whoever *believes* in Him should not perish but have everlasting life." John 3:36 continues, "He who *believes* in the Son has everlasting life ..." The majority of the 101 derivatives of the word "believe" used by John in his Gospel refer to salvation by believing in Jesus.

We must remember that the people John was writing to didn't have the New Testament and the whole Bible as we do today. Yet his only emphasis to initiate salvation was to focus them to simply believe on Jesus.

Even though John never mentioned repentance, his Gospel by its essence changed the peoples' thinking from what they previously believed would take away their sins to, "Behold! The Lamb of God who takes away the sin of the world!" (John 1:29). Repentance in John's Gospel is a given. In order to believe on Jesus we must turn to Him.

John states again in his first epistle that the assurance of Jesus' saving grace is inseparable from our belief in Him. He says, "These things I have written to you who *believe* in the name of the Son of God, *that you may know* that you have eternal life and that you may continue to *believe* in the name of the Son of God" (1 John 5:13 emphasis added).

Most people who lack this kind of assurance have mixed their "belief in Jesus" with something else to form their foundation. Repenting (changing our thinking) caused us to turn and believe in Jesus. Even this "repentance," which is part of the salvation process, in a sense, has nothing do to with us—it is a part of God's wonderful grace toward us.

7

Immediately following the day of Pentecost, Peter said, "Him [Jesus] God has exalted to His right hand to be Prince and Savior, *to give repentance* to Israel and forgiveness of sins" (Acts 5:31 emphasis added). Even this repentance toward salvation is not of ourselves—otherwise we would be able to boast (see Ephesians 2:8–9). We don't even have the ability to turn to God for salvation without Him giving it to us. What an awesome love God has for us to allow us to turn and believe on Jesus.

When asked the question, "Who is the one who repents of sin?" we cannot respond any other way than to say ourselves. In this case, it must not be added as part of the foundation for our salvation, because this process is something that we do.

If there is any part of us in the foundation, whether it is our works, our feelings, our repentance of sin, etc., we will always feel insecure and have cause to doubt. The inferior material of our lives cannot do anything but weaken the steadfast permanence of faith's foundation. When our faith is planted firmly on Jesus and Him only, we never have reason to doubt its permanence.

Only Believe

Believing in Jesus is like the reinforcement rods that hold our life to Him so we have a truly firm foundation. Therefore, to place our lives on the foundation of Jesus, all we need do initially is to turn to Him and believe.

Leja Messenger was once a Russian baroness with a 300-room castle, who in recent years lived in Michigan. The ex-baroness met God in a remarkable way just before the Russian revolution.

When the Germans invaded Russia in 1914 (and her husband went off to war) Leja Messenger was left in charge of the castle—which the Russian Red Cross commandeered as a hospital for wounded troops. One day, the baroness admitted stretcher-bearers carrying a young boy, about fifte, covered with bloody rags. A shell explosion had exposed both his skull and lungs and it seemed a miracle that he was alive. The bearers placed him in the great ballroom and the baroness knelt beside him.

Realizing that he was dying, she asked if he had a last message. "No last message, lady," he said, "but would you help me pray?" The baroness panicked. Not knowing how to pray herself, she looked around frantically for a priest but saw none. She thought of the Lord's Prayer but could not remember the words. "Too late," he moaned. "I'm lost. I'm lost." He kept repeating the words.

As the baroness now remembers, "I felt I was dying too. Then suddenly as if my brain cells were saying words I didn't recognize at first, I was saying the words of John 3:16 [a nun had taught her this verse in a girls' school]. God was prompting me." The boy's face lighted briefly, then he moaned again. "Too late. I'm lost." As if in a trance, the baroness heard herself speak. "Didn't you hear? Whosoever believeth in Him shall not perish, but have everlasting life. You must believe before it is too late."

While she begged the boy to believe, her own heart was changed. Now she says, "He died believing in Jesus Christ. I lived believing. God came to me at that moment and revealed Himself."[4]

This is a remarkable true story of "only believe."

The Foundation Laid in Acts

When we study the Word of God to find examples of how people were saved, it is quite amazing. The first account of Jewish people being saved is found in Acts 2. It is astounding to hear so many Christians quoting the last phrase of Acts 2:37, "Men and brethren, what shall we do *to be saved*?" This verse, no matter what translation you read, does not contain those last three underlined words. It simply says, "What shall we do?"

People, as a result of these "tagged on" words, look to verse 38 in order to show how people are "saved." It says, "Repent and let every one of you be baptized in the name of Jesus Christ for the remission of sins; and you shall receive the gift of the Holy Spirit."

This, however, is not the way these Jewish people were saved. As Peter was preaching about Jesus and who He really was, verse 37 took place: "Now when they heard this they were cut to the heart and said to Peter and the rest of the Apostles, 'Men and brethren, what shall we do?'" At precisely the moment Peter was preaching, they came to believe what he was saying concerning Jesus. When they discovered that they had crucified Jesus, the Messiah, the One who came to save them, they were cut to the heart. In essence, they believed in Jesus at that very point in time. After they believed and knew what they had done, they then said, "What shall we do?" This is where repentance, baptism and receiving the Holy Spirit follow.

The verse that people quote, "What must I do to be saved?" was actually said by the Philippian jailer (Acts 16:30). Paul's response to this question is, "Believe on the Lord Jesus Christ and you will be saved" (Acts 16:31). Paul then spoke the Word of the Lord to him and his entire household. After this they were baptized and had something to eat and, the Bible concludes, "he rejoiced, having believed in God with all his household" (Acts 16:34).

The first account of Gentiles being saved is very similar to that of the Jews. Peter was preaching the words, "To Him all the prophets witness that, through His name, whoever believes in Him will receive remission of sins. While Peter was still speaking these words, the Holy Spirit fell upon all those who heard the word" (Acts 10:43–44). Peter didn't make an altar call or lead them in a prayer (although I believe very much in doing both), they simply believed in Jesus as Peter was preaching. As a result, they were filled with the Holy Spirit and then commanded to be water baptized.

Jesus completed our salvation on the Cross. He said, "It is finished." The atoning work of Calvary was complete and entire; we could add nothing to it. "For by grace you have been saved through faith, and that not of yourselves: it is the gift of God, not of works, lest anyone should boast" (Ephesians 2:8–9). The foundation of our faith rests totally on Jesus and Him alone, not by how much we do or feel or any such thing. If it did rest even somewhat on us, we would have great reason to doubt, question and feel insecure, but it doesn't at all.

The words of a great hymn by Reverend E. Mite and W. B. Bradbury say it all:

My hope is built on nothing less
Than Jesus' blood and righteousness.
I dare not trust the sweetest frame
But wholly lean on Jesus' name.
On Christ the solid Rock I stand,
All other ground is sinking sand.

Make sure the foundation for your salvation is Jesus and Him alone. This is the first step to building your life in God.

Some find it difficult to grasp that we don't have to do anything in order to have a secure foundation.

Let me ask you a question to explain why it must be so simple. What did you do in order to receive your sinful nature? You would probably say absolutely nothing, other than to be born. That is exactly correct. You obtained it when you were born into Adam's lineage. Now, Jesus came as the "second Adam" and it is exactly the same with Him. There is nothing we can do in order to have Jesus' righteous nature but be born again into His lineage by believing in Him.

Paul paints this wonderful picture while writing to the Romans. He says, "Therefore, as through one man's offense judgment came to all men, resulting in condemnation, even so through one Man's righteous act the free gift came to all men, resulting in justification of life" (Romans 5:18). Our nature, whether sinful or righteous, depends on the single act of another: Adam or Jesus, and which lineage we are born into.

You and I can do nothing to secure our eternal life. It has been completely secured by Jesus and Him alone. If Jesus has secured it, why do we ever doubt it? Our insecurity is usually because we think some part of salvation rests on us and we cannot trust ourselves.

The rich young ruler came to Jesus and asked Him, "Good Teacher, *what good thing shall I do* that I may have eternal life?" (Matthew 19:16 emphasis added). The young man wanted to know what he had to do for salvation. After Jesus' conversation with him, he went away grieved, because he wasn't prepared to do what Jesus asked.

The disciples then questioned Jesus after hearing Him speak about those who could enter the kingdom of God. They wondered, "Who then can be saved?" Jesus replied, "With men this is impossible, but with God all things are possible" (Matthew 19:26). Salvation is impossible for any person to achieve, because only God can do it for us. We can't dare trust in any way our ability for salvation, for it is impossible for us. We are only to "have faith in God."

What tremendous security we have in this! Words do not do justice to express how secure and trustworthy God is. Paul says, "Much more then, having now been justified by His blood, we shall be saved from wrath through Him. For if when we were enemies we were reconciled to God through the death of His Son, how much more, having been reconciled we shall be saved by His life" (Romans 5:9–10).

We are safe and secure in God when we put our trust in Him and not in ourselves. After Jesus had talked to some of the Jews at the Feast of Dedication about not believing in Him, He finished with the following words:

My sheep hear My voice and I know them and they follow Me. And I give them eternal life and they shall never perish, neither shall anyone snatch them out of My hand.

12

My Father, who has given them to Me, is greater than all, and no one is able to snatch them out of My Father's hand (John 10:27–29).

What an awesome promise to believe and trust. Jesus doesn't just save us, He holds on to us. In the first *Superman* movie, Lois Lane's initial encounter with Superman is when she is plummeting from a building. Superman flies up to catch her at about the halfway point of her descent. Superman says, "Don't worry Miss, I've got you." Lois responds in utter amazement, "You've got me, but who's got you?"

We are totally safe and secure in God's hands. We need never doubt Him. How could, or why would anyone want to doubt the One who has done and will do everything to see us safely home to heaven?

God says it is His will that none should perish. What else does He do? The writer of Hebrews says, "He is also able to save to the uttermost those who come to God through Him, since He always lives to make intercession for them" (Hebrews 7:25).

Once a person believes, Jesus doesn't just leave him there, He continues to intercede for him right from that very moment until the end (the uttermost). Have you ever doubted that God the Father would refuse to answer one of Jesus' prayers? No. In that case, we have a sure and certain hope to build upon, which eliminates doubt.

I believe doubt is the primary reason many Christians lack confidence in serving God. They are so busy trying to keep their lives in God when, in fact, He is willing and more than able to keep each one of us, when our faith is in Him. We need to continually look to Jesus not only as the author but as the "finisher of our faith" as well (Hebrews 12:2).

The Right Emphasis for Salvation

If there is one other area we must look at carefully concerning the foundation of our salvation, it is that of confession or praying. It's so important that people seeking salvation are instructed with the correct emphasis. In Romans 10, Paul shares specifically about this subject. Let's look at it in detail.

Many walk the altars of our churches or pray a "sinner's prayer" to be saved. We need to ask ourselves some tough questions about why a number of these people do not continue in the faith. I believe it is because of where we have placed the emphasis for salvation. Two scriptures in Romans 10 direct us toward getting people to confess the Lord Jesus in order to be saved:

- That if you confess with your mouth the Lord Jesus and believe in your heart that God has raised Him from the dead, you will be saved (Romans 10:9).
- For whoever calls on the name of the LORD shall be saved (Romans 10:13).

As we read the subsequent two verses of these scriptures in context, we find they highlight for us the right perspective and proper emphasis:

- For with the *heart* one *believes* unto righteousness (Romans 10:10 emphasis added).
- How then shall they *call on Him in whom they have not believed*? (Romans 10:14a emphasis added).

We have shared much on believing in Jesus. These scriptures clarify where belief comes from—the heart, not the mouth. Even though Romans 10:13 says "whoever calls upon the name of the LORD shall be saved", the subsequent verse says we can't call upon Him *until* we have believed. Jesus further warns us, "Not everyone who *says to me Lord, Lord* shall enter the kingdom of heaven" (Matthew 7:21 emphasis added).

R.C. Sproul makes a very true statement similar to "it is not *our confession* of faith that saves us, but *our possession* of faith in Jesus." Once we possess faith we can't help but profess it, for "faith believes and therefore speaks" (2 Corinthians 4:13). Only a handful of scriptures in the New Testament address *confession* in conjunction with salvation. Whereas it would be near impossible to find one without *belief*.

Can I implore you, that whenever you share the gospel with people that your goal is to work with the Holy Spirit in order for them to believe "in their heart" what Jesus has done for them? Then you'll be hard-pressed holding them back from professing their faith with both their mouth and lifestyle.

Personally, you may need to look at your foundation again and see Jesus and your belief in Him as the only substance. Be confident that your life is now built firmly on Him and Him alone.

CHAPTER 2

LEARNING RIGHTEOUSNESS

For more than six hundred years the Hapsburgs exercised political power in Europe. When Emperor Franz-Josef I of Austria died in 1916, his was the last of the extravagant imperial funerals.

A processional of dignitaries and elegantly-dressed court personages escorted the coffin, draped in the black and gold imperial colors. To the accompaniment of a military band's somber dirges and by the light of torches, the cortegé descended the stairs of the Capuchin Monastery in Vienna. At the bottom was a great iron door leading to the Hapsburg family crypt. Behind the door was the Cardinal-Archbishop of Vienna.

The officer in charge followed the prescribed ceremony, established centuries before. "Open!" he cried.

"Who goes there?" responded the Cardinal.

"We bear the remains of his Imperial and Apostolic Majesty, Franz-Josef I, by the grace of God Emperor of Austria, King of Hungary, Defender of the Faith, Prince of Bohemia-Moravia, Grand Duke of Lombardy, Venezia, Styrgia ..." The officer continued to list the Emperor's thirty-seven titles.

17

"We know him not," replied the Cardinal. "Who goes there?"

The officer spoke again, this time using a much abbreviated and less ostentatious title reserved for times of expediency.

"We know him not," the Cardinal said again. "Who goes there?"

The officer tried a third time, stripping the emperor of all but the humblest of titles: "We bear the body of Franz-Josef, our brother, a sinner like us all!"

At that, the doors swung open, and Franz-Josef was admitted.[5]

Most of us believe that we have led reasonably good lives. We haven't done some of the horrendous things others have done. We could honestly say that many of the wrong things we have done were never intended to hurt God or others. In fact, we have often corrected ourselves after doing something wrong. We have also resisted myriads of tempting thoughts. By and large, we have done very well in living reasonably good lifestyles.

With this kind of thinking we have lulled ourselves into a false sense of security. We don't just compare ourselves to an average human standard. We usually judge ourselves by the extremity of what human beings are "capable of doing."

Consider now that most worldly courts no longer consider adultery, homosexuality and sexual activity before marriage convictable offenses. They aren't even deemed to be minor offenses. It is little wonder we don't have a great understanding of sin.

The Gravity of Sin

Humanity fails to think or dwell upon the consequences of its sin because it can't believe its sin is bad enough to deserve the total wrath of God. All people compare their sin with the worst of others' sins. They can't see that their "little sins" deserve the same kind of punishment.

As long as we hold views like these, we will never truly understand why God punishes sin. We will always see Him as unfair and unjust and never be able to truly comprehend God as He really is. We will formulate a "god" in our own "Christian concept" that isn't really the God of the universe. If we reduce the justice and the fairness of God, we will also reduce the love God demonstrated by sacrificing Jesus for us.

In the same proportion that we fail to understand the gravity of our sin, we will also fail to know and understand the love God has for us.

Just Consequences of Sin

Some comparisons of Old Testament law with today:

Type of Sin	Reference	Old Testament Consequence	Consequence Today
Advice from a medium	Lev. 20:6	Cut off from God's people	No crime
Curse father or mother	Lev. 20:9	Put to death	Protected by Child Welfare at times
Committing adultery	Lev. 20:10	Put to death	Free to re-marry
Homosexuality	Lev. 20:13	Put to death	Protected by anti-discrimination laws
Becoming a medium	Lev. 20:27	Put to death	Good living from profits
Using God's name in vain	Lev. 24:16	Stoned to death	Common language
Loosing virginity before marriage	Deut. 22:20–21	Stoned to death	Very common

I do not in any way suggest that we go back under Old Testament law, but I use these consequences only as a comparison to show the severity of God's punishment compared to what society today doesn't even call misdemeanors. Today our society fosters many of these sins with its protection.

I do not judge any person who may have done any of these things or the myriads of others I haven't listed. Taking a paper clip from work without permission was enough to sentence Jesus to die in my stead.

The punishment God assigned to specific sins in the Old Testament gives us some idea of the gravity of sin. Think further—just one of your fleeting, lustful thoughts or just one of the times you gossiped was enough for the innocent life of Jesus to be sentenced to death for you. Just one of the most insignificant sins was enough for God to condemn Jesus to die a horrendous death in our place. He suffered the full extent of God's wrath for each and every one of our sins.

Jacob Marcellus Kik, editor of *Bible Christianity*, preached a sermon on the cup of Gethsemane. He said:

The cup from which the soul of Jesus shrank with horror was a cup filled with the sin of the world. In that cup were the guilt and the pollution of sin. In that cup He could see the totality of sin, with all its length and width and depth. Just think! The world's sin with all its length and width and depth! One may talk about the brutality of a Joseph Stalin. In that cup was the brutality of a thousand Stalins. One may shrink from the filthiness of sexual deviates. In that cup was the filthiness of a thousand sexual deviates. The sin of atheism, of idolatry, of profanity, of Sabbath-breaking, of disobedience to parents, of murder, of adultery, of stealing, of bearing false witness, and of covetousness—your sins and mine—they were all in the cup that confronted Jesus in Gethsemane.

A person may well feel oppressed by the weight of his own sin and guilt. But think about the weight of the whole world's sin and guilt. All of that sin pressed upon the soul of Christ in the Garden.[6]

God's love for you and I was so great that He wouldn't remove the cup of sin or the cup of His wrath from Jesus. Instead, He poured out both cups in all their fullness upon Him for you and I. I don't think that we are able to fully comprehend how heinous sin really is. To think that stealing a pen from work or lying to a parent was enough for God to rightly and justly banish us to hell for all eternity seems impossible to understand. Our thoughts don't usually let us go past this point, but try to think how much God must loathe sin. How much must sin hurt Him?

We Are Not a Victim

It is easy for us to think of ourselves as victims of a harsh and cruel and unfair God who exaggerates our punishment beyond belief. At times we are so self-centered with regard to this area—the "poor me" who wasn't really wanting to do something wrong, but was tempted by the 'someone' who really deserves the punishment. We self-righteously say we may have done the actual deed, however, this harsh God is wrong for blaming and punishing us.

We need to understand we are not victims, but criminals who commit crimes against God, who is the innocent victim.

The devil, in a most incredible sequence of events, leads us to destruction. First, he tempts us to commit sin. Second, he accuses us of doing something wrong before God and, finally, he tells us that God is unjust in giving us the punishment we deserve.

You can't get a more insane sequence of events, which we not only follow but also believe.

It is rare to hear children or criminals state that they deserved the full punishment for what they did wrong. I remember hearing of a person who visited a prison and came out saying he had never met so many innocent people.

Admitting Guilt

When we won't admit that we are the offenders, it closes the door to God's grace. "God resists the proud, but gives grace to the humble" (James 4:6).

After coming to an awareness of sin and how anti-God sin is, we can then understand and comprehend God's judgment of sin. It is only when we see God's total justice in His judgment of sin that we can then begin to learn His righteousness.

On the Cross, justice and mercy were both seen. On the Cross, judgment and righteousness were also both revealed. The Apostle Paul makes one of the most profound and powerful statements concerning the gospel. He said:

> For I am not ashamed of the gospel of Christ, for it is the power of God to salvation for everyone who believes, for in it the *righteousness of God is revealed* ... for the *wrath of God is revealed* from heaven against all ungodliness and unrighteousness of men (Romans 1:16–18 emphasis added).

Two things are revealed: righteousness and wrath (judgment). Notice Paul didn't say, "the wrath of God is revealed from heaven against all ungodly and unrighteous men," for then not one person on the face of the planet would be able to survive. Instead the verse says, Jesus took the wrath for all the "ungodliness and unrighteousness *of* man," speaking of our sinful acts and nature.

When we understand God's just judgment and punishment for our sin, then and only then can we begin to comprehend the gift of love and righteousness He has given us. Then and only then will we see His unfathomable forgiveness and grace. From this point we will be able to respond to Him and to life with a hatred for sin and a love for righteousness.

Grace Alone Doesn't Induce Righteousness

A story is told about a man who was in a supermarket with his two-year-old son. The little boy kept pulling everything he could get his hands on from the shelves. The father would replace the item and say, "Calm yourself, Ronnie." The boy would run away and hit the other customers and he father would say, "Calm yourself, Ronnie."

When they were going through the checkout line, the little boy toppled a whole candy display and the father said, "Calm yourself, Ronnie."

Finally, one of the customers, having taken as much as she could stand, said to the father, "Sir, your little boy is a brat. He needs a good swift kick in the pants, and all you can say is, 'Calm yourself, Ronnie.'"

"Madam," the father answered, "you don't understand. My boy's name is Mike. I'm Ronnie."

Isaiah, one of the great Old Testament prophets wrote, "Let grace be shown to the wicked, Yet he will not learn righteousness; In the land of uprightness he will deal unjustly, And will not behold the majesty of the LORD" (Isaiah 26:10).

Many lives have been shown the grace of God but, sadly, never learn righteousness. They continue to be just as sinful and ungodly as they were before they were given grace. These people come into Christian circles and pollute the church with their unjust dealings. We tend to continue pouring out the grace of God upon them hoping that they will "change." Our efforts will continually be thwarted because they haven't seen the total work of the Cross.

The key to learning righteousness is found in Isaiah's previous verse. It says, "For when Your judgments are in the earth, The inhabitants of the world will learn righteousness" (Isaiah 26:9).

These people who are shown the grace of God but continue in all manner of sin have never learned righteousness because they didn't see the judgment of God first. Unless they see the debasement of their sin and God's punishment of it in Jesus on the Cross, they will never behold His awesome majesty and forgiveness.

In order for a person to properly appropriate the grace of God in his life, he must first see the judgment of his sin in Jesus on the Cross.

To Whom Much Is Forgiven

By far the greatest key I have found to establishing Christians in their faith and relationship with God is a seemingly insignificant statement Jesus made to Simon the Pharisee.

Jesus had just been accused of being a friend of tax collectors and sinners because He spent a considerable amount of time eating and drinking with them. One of the Pharisees named Simon, decided to invite Jesus to his place for a meal. As Jesus sat down to eat, a woman whom they knew to be a notable sinner came in. She sat at Jesus' feet and began to wash them with her tears and dry them with her hair. After she finished, she anointed His feet with fragrant oil from an alabaster box.

While she had been doing this, Simon was thinking to himself, "This man, if He were a prophet, would know who and what manner of woman this is who is touching Him, for she is a sinner" (Luke 7:39). Jesus, perceiving what Simon was thinking in his heart, said, "Simon, I have something to say to you" (Luke 7:40). Jesus then proceeded to speak a parable concerning a creditor who had two debtors. By today's values one owed about $60,000 and the other $6,000.

Jesus asked Simon a question. If the creditor forgave both of the debts, "Tell Me, therefore, which of them will love him more?" Simon answered correctly, "The one who was forgiven more." Jesus then begins to admonish Simon for all the things Simon should have done that the sinful woman had done in his house. At the very end, Jesus makes this statement: "Therefore I say to you, her sins, which are many, are forgiven, for she loved much. But to whom little is forgiven, the same loves little" (Luke 7:47).

This is one of the most vital aspects for the start of a Christian's life and it is found in the statement, "But to whom little is forgiven, the same loves little." In the same proportion people know how much they have been forgiven, will they love and serve God.

It is not the grossness of specific sins that Jesus is talking about—"We have all sinned and fallen short of the glory of God" (Romans 3:23). If we have sinned in one point of the Law we are guilty of all. It is the gravity of redemption, and how much forgiveness we have received, that we need to understand.

Think deeply about the suffering and judgment of God that was placed on Jesus for our sins. What an awesome God we have; what incredible love He has for you and I. We remember just a drop in the bucket of all the sins that we have committed against Him. We must allow our knowledge and awareness of the gravity of His forgiveness to deepen.

With the same proportion we understand this, we will love and serve God. When I first saw this about five years ago, it really challenged me. I said to God, "Reveal to me afresh, how much you have forgiven me, so I can love you all the more." New and old Christians alike must become aware of this. They must come to an understanding of how much God has forgiven them. The measure with which they see God's forgiveness, will be the measure with which they will love and serve God.

I believe that Paul was arguably the greatest of all the apostles. You may ask, "Why do I think that?" In First Timothy 1:15, Paul says to Timothy, "This is a faithful saying and worthy of all acceptance, that Christ Jesus came into the world to save sinners, of whom I am chief." I believe Paul was the greatest, because he saw himself as the chief of all sinners. When he saw himself this way, he couldn't help but see God had forgiven him the most of all who had lived. It was in the same proportion that he went on to love and serve God.

If we build this understanding within our hearts and lives and build it within the lives of the people we desire to disciple, we will see them stand on one of the greatest premises for building their lives. We will not have to motivate ourselves or others to love and serve God, but will be compelled by God's great love for us. You will not have to prompt, goad or twist others' arms to love God. If they understand the depths of God's forgiveness, they will love Him with all of their heart.

Let this truth burn within your heart and life. Paul's love for God and his willingness to serve Him is within the realm of human achievement. We, can love Christ as Paul did, when we know how much we've been forgiven.

Understanding Forgiveness

Whatever the stage of our Christian walk, it is vital that we comprehend these two statements concerning forgiveness:

When Your judgments are in the earth, The inhabitants of the world will learn righteousness (Isaiah 26:9).

To whom much is forgiven the same will love much. To whom little is forgiven the same loves little (Luke 3:47).

These are two of the foundational principles of the gospel. We will live our lives for God, with the same proportion we understand and give ourselves to these truths. Christians who apply these truths need little encouragement to continue on in faith, steadfast to the end, for they grasp the depravity and grossness of sin and also the incredible love and forgiveness of God towards them.

Without understanding the depravity, grossness and judgment of sin, we never understand the love, acceptance and forgiveness of God. Through receiving and understanding the love and forgiveness of God, we can love and serve Him in the capacity He deserves.

CHAPTER 3

BELIEVING UNTO SALVATION

For many years one of the primary purposes of our church and churches around the world has been to see people born again. I want to broaden our minds a little and challenge our thinking concerning salvation.

Jesus' primary purpose was and still is to "seek and save the lost." He also put forth a warning to those who initially called Him "Lord," but didn't follow through. He said, "Not everyone who says Lord, Lord, shall enter the kingdom of heaven, but he who does the will of my Father which is in heaven" (Matthew 7:21).

There are several questions we need to ask ourselves and those who come to believe in Jesus concerning salvation. What is the real focus of salvation? How do we truly obtain salvation? What do we each believe concerning our salvation and the salvation of others?

Salvation in Perspective

Let's look at a few scriptures concerning salvation to give us a proper perspective on the subject.

First, Jesus is both the author and finisher of faith. Hebrews 12:2 says, "Looking unto Jesus, the author and the finisher of our faith." The primary focus of this verse is Jesus. In Him is the whole spectrum of a person's faith from beginning to end. Sadly, many people who come to believe in Jesus only get to first base.

Second, the initial act of believing does not necessarily produce salvation in totality. A number of scriptures highlight this fact. Romans 13:11 (KJV) says, "now is our *salvation nearer* than when we *believed.*" 1 Peter 1:5 (KJV) says, "Who are kept by the power of God though faith *unto* salvation." Verse 9 (KJV) continues: "Receiving the *end*, of your faith, *even* the salvation of your souls." God draws a startling distinction through verses like these, emphasizing that salvation is the culmination of both the beginning and the end of our faith, not just the commencing.

Jude gives us a very clear warning when he says, "I want to remind you, though you once knew this, that the Lord, having saved the people out of the land of Egypt, afterward destroyed those who did not believe" (Jude 5). These Israelites had already performed the initial act of believing when they obeyed God in offering the Passover (placing the blood on the door posts and lintels of their homes). The result was being protected from the angel of death as He passed over them. Then they all went through the Red Sea and the cloud; this spoke of baptism. They all ate the same spiritual food and drank the same spiritual drink, speaking of Christ (1 Corinthians 10:1–3). After God had saved them and kept them for forty years, He couldn't take them into the Promised Land because of their unbelief. He had to destroy them.

I have a friend, Angela Harris, whom I have known for twenty-one years. Before she was married to her husband, Garry, her name was Angela Russell. She was the Australian 50-meter freestyle champion and record holder for seven years. Angela was also a multiple medallist at the Brisbane and Edinburgh Commonwealth Games.

During 1983, Angela left school to focus on achieving her dream of competing at the 1984 Olympic Games in Los Angeles.

There was no 50-meter race at this Olympics, so Angela would have to move up to the 100-meter event. For this preparation she trained with legendary swimming coach, Laurie Lawrence.

Laurie broke down Angela's race into its five major sections: Angela needed an explosive start, she needed speed over the first fifty meters, a great turn, strength for the second fifty meters and, finally, a precision touch on the wall.

If Laurie only had Angela focus on the start and never told her to focus on the whole race, where would she have gone? How fast would she have swum? Would she have even finished the race?

Devastatingly, many new Christians never finish the race because their coach only has them focus on the start and then leaves them to wander aimlessly on their own.

All the groundwork had been done by Angela and her coach before it came time to commence her race. Angela knew exactly what she had to do: start the race well, pace herself well and finish well. All stages of the race had to be executed with precision.

Angela's training paid off; she was selected to represent Australia at the Los Angeles Olympics. When the day arrived, Angela was introduced to the crowd along with seven other young ladies in her heat, all aspiring to be in the final that night.

The eight young ladies took to their blocks, eyes fixed toward the end of the pool. The starter told them to take their marks and, in a matter of seconds, the starter's gun signaled their launch into the pool. What were the results?

Angela won her heat in a personal best time of 57.14 seconds and made the final by the smallest possible margin of .01 seconds. The final was won in a dead heat by the two American swimmers, the first time an Olympic gold medal was shared. Although Angela finished out of the medals, she claimed her piece of Olympic history.

If Angela was only instructed to commence the race, but not told how to finish, she would never have won her heat and reached the final. Consider how disappointed in her coach Angela would have been if she was only told to dive into the water and nothing more. After her dive, she would have come to the surface, looked around, and seen many of the others swimming for their lives. She would have been oblivious to the goal of reaching the pool's end in the best possible time.

Angela would probably have gotten out of the water at the nearest side, thinking that she had done all she was supposed to do, none the wiser that it, in fact, was a race. She would not have finished, and the results, when posted on the electronic screen with the letters "DQ" appearing beside her name, would mean that she was disqualified. Her disqualification would be warranted because she exited the pool without finishing the race.

How many people do we know who were instructed to begin the Christian life, but never told that finishing was of the utmost of importance? Jesus made a very clear statement concerning faith. He said, "He who endures to the end shall be saved" (Matthew 24:13). Ending the race is paramount if we are to receive our prize. It is not enough to believe in the "pearl of great price." Even the devils believe and tremble but they are far from being saved. We must coach and disciple each other to the end of the race, not just instruct on how to start.

In Second Corinthians 11:2 the Apostle Paul said, "I am jealous over you with a godly jealousy for I have espoused you to one husband that I may present you as a chaste virgin to Christ." We must jealously guard and watch over other Christians' lives.

Paul instructed Timothy in a similar manner to "Take heed to yourself and to the doctrine. *Continue* in them, for in doing this you will save both yourself and those who hear you" (1 Timothy 4:16 emphasis added).

What a joy it will be to come to Jesus and say, "Here they are, Jesus. Here is my brother, here is my sister. Here is my mother, here is my father. Here is my friend, here is my work colleague. Here they are. I've been jealously watching over them for you, Jesus. I didn't just want to introduce them to you; I wanted to present them to you." First Thessalonians 2:19–20 says, "For what is our hope or joy or crown of rejoicing? Is it not even you in the presence of our Lord Jesus Christ at His coming? For you are our glory and joy."

Coach Laurie Lawrence celebrated with Angela on that day. Although Angela didn't receive a medal, she did receive a certificate for her achievement. Laurie was there to rejoice with her. This was his whole goal, to see Angela at the end, receiving her prize. We have no greater joy than to see the ones we care for and love standing there with us at the end. This is our joy. This is our crown of rejoicing. This is our glory and our hope. This is our goal, to see them with us at the very end with Jesus.

In Colossians 1:28, Paul says, "Him we preach, warning every man and teaching every man in all wisdom, that we may present every man perfect in Christ Jesus. To this end I also labor, striving according to His working which works in me mightily."

To present every man perfect in Christ—what a goal! Our goal is to look at every single person we're going to lead to the Lord and every single person that we're going to disciple and see us presenting them "perfect" to Jesus. If they follow us and we're following the Lord, then we're going to take them to the end of the race and to that finishing place.

The Start

The start of any race is very important, but the start of the Christian's life is vital. If Angela didn't get off to a good start in that race, she wouldn't have done her personal best.

In Acts 20 we read about Paul's final address to the church at Ephesus before heading to Jerusalem. Some of his concluding remarks reveal how he ministered to them. He said he ministered to them by "serving the Lord with all humility, with many tears and trials which happened to me by the plotting of the Jews; how I kept back nothing that was helpful, but proclaimed it to you publicly and from house to house, testifying to the Jews, and also to Greeks, repentance toward God and faith toward our Lord Jesus Christ" (Acts 20:19–21).

The last verse identifies two parts to sharing the gospel. The first is repentance toward God. The second is faith towards our Lord Jesus Christ. If we don't have these two parts then the start will never happen. In Luke 24:47, Jesus says, "repentance and remission of sin should be preached in His name among all nations beginning in Jerusalem."

People must have both repentance and faith in coming to Jesus. I mentioned in chapter one that "repentance of sin" was not to be added into the foundation; however, I also mentioned that "repentance toward God" was distinctively different from "repentance of sin."

To believe in Jesus requires the two elements of repentance and faith. Faith in Jesus implies that a person must first see his inability to make amends with God by himself and therefore repent (change his mind) toward God's plan of redemption through faith in what Jesus has done.

Romans 3:24 says, "The law is the Schoolmaster to bring us to Christ." The Law shows us our sinfulness and the punishment we deserve for our sin. The Law makes it very clear to us that there is no way we can be right with God through our own merit, hence bringing us to Jesus, the only one who can cause this to take place.

The Holy Spirit through the Law convicts us that we have sinned and have been separated from God. Once convicted, our hearts can be humbled enough to change our minds about our self-righteousness and we can become recipients of God's wonderful grace. For faith to be shared with us this must first take place; the Law must expose the sinful state of our lives.

In chapter two we saw that if grace was shown to a wicked man, he would not learn righteousness. God's grace can only come through faith, but faith can't come until repentance toward God has first been established. In reality, both of these aspects can take place in a matter of moments, but the order of how it transpires is vital.

Notice the following two examples of Jesus sharing with others about eternal life.

The Despair of the Rich Young Ruler

The rich young ruler came to Jesus and asked Him, "Good master, what must I do to inherit the kingdom of God?" From this one question alone, Jesus understood where the young man was coming from. Jesus answered him by saying there is no one good enough to make it to heaven on his own. He then proceeded to show him his performance could never match up in reality.

Jesus instructed the young ruler to keep the commandments in order to inherit the kingdom. The young man asked, "Which ones?" Jesus then replied by mentioning six of them. The response came, "All these things I have kept from my youth" (Matthew 19:20).

If the young ruler thought he had eternal life already, he would never have asked Jesus the question in the first place, but even after Jesus instructs him in what to do to have eternal life, the answer still isn't resolved within his being. According to his response he has done everything that was necessary, but he still doesn't have an assurance on the inside. He still feels that something is missing.

The young man then puts another question to Jesus, "What do I still lack?" Jesus further said to him, "Go sell what you have and give it to the poor, and you will have treasure in heaven; and come, follow Me" (Matthew 19:21). The young man, as a result, went away grieved in his heart without any assurance.

What was the process Jesus used?

First, Jesus tried to point out that no one is good enough in himself to enter into eternal life.

Second, He brought the young ruler to the Law, but the Law never convicted him of his sin. It only confirmed the self-righteous state of his heart.

33

Third, Jesus, the Word Himself, gave another commandment for the young man to obey. Conviction obviously came to his heart at that point, but it never brought him to a place of repentance and he walked away grieved.

You and I, at that point, would probably have run off after him saying, "Hey, come back here. Let me share with you some more. Don't go away yet. I need to share with you that Jesus loves you. He died on the Cross for you."

It would have made no difference whatsoever to that person because he never came to a place of conviction and repentance within his heart.

Good news is not good news to those who don't recognize their need for it. Unless we bring them to that place of repentance (turning to Jesus and following Him) first, we can never share with them the good news of having faith in Jesus.

Jesus never shared the good news with the rich young ruler or any of the self-righteous Pharisees. Why? Because they never came to the place of repentance or turning toward God for their righteousness.

The Jubilation of Zacchaeus

On the other hand, look at what happens to Zacchaeus in Luke 19:1–10. There he was, sitting up in the tree. Jesus walked down the road and saw him and said, "Zacchaeus, come down, I want to have lunch with you today."

Zacchaeus came down and walked with Jesus back to his home. The Bible doesn't record what Jesus talked to Zacchaeus about, but the response of Zacchaeus gives us a good idea as to what might have been said.

By all indications Zacchaeus was at home when he said to Jesus, "Look, Lord, I give half of my goods to the poor; and if I have taken anything from anyone by false accusation, I restore them fourfold" (Luke 19:8). According to the King James and New King James Versions of the Bible, the word "fourfold" is only recorded twice. It is a very strong possibility that Zacchaeus had a precedent in using "fourfold" in restitution.

King David used the term in Second Samuel 12:1–13. The Lord had sent Nathan to bring about a confession from David concerning his sin in respect to Uriah and Bathsheba. Nathan started his address with the statement, "There were two men in one city, one rich and the other poor." So far it could be seen as a correlation with Zacchaeus' situation. Nathan goes on further to say that the rich man had unlawfully taken from the poor man. David's response is passionate, saying that the rich man should die for this crime and also restore to the poor man fourfold.

David then discovers that he is the man who has done this. While he spent time with Jesus, Zacchaeus discovered he had done likewise. In Second Samuel 12:13 David said to Nathan, "I have sinned against the Lord" to which Nathan responded, "The LORD also has put away your sin; you shall not die."

Once Zacchaeus had stated his intention concerning what he would do with his money, Jesus made a similar statement to him:

Today salvation has come to this house, because he is also a son of Abraham; for the Son of Man has come to seek and to save that which is lost (Luke 19:9–10).

Jesus' statement seems like a contradiction of terms. He said that salvation came because Zacchaeus was a "son of Abraham," but then He goes on to say that He came to "seek and save the lost." If being a "son of Abraham" meant that Abraham's natural offspring would be saved, then why did Jesus add that He came to "seek and save the lost?" Zacchaeus, being an Israelite (the natural offspring of Abraham), shouldn't have been lost in the first place.

The only explanation for these two statements to flow together is that being a "son of Abraham" means to "believe God." Romans 4:3 says, "Abraham believed God, and it was accounted to him for righteousness." Verse eleven goes on to say that Abraham was "the father of all those who believe."

In the same passage of scripture, Paul writes concerning the forgiveness David received from God:

> But to him who does not work but believes on Him who justifies the ungodly, his faith is accounted for righteousness, just as David also describes the blessedness of the man to whom God imputes righteousness apart from works" (Romans 4:5–6).

Zacchaeus, somewhere in his conversation with Jesus, was convicted that he was a sinner. Even though Zacchaeus sought to make restitution for his sins toward others, according to Jesus, he primarily "believed God." It was this faith that led Jesus to say to him, "Today salvation has come to this house." Following is a synopsis of the stories.

Topic	Rich Young Ruler	Zacchaeus
Financial status	Rich	Rich
Eternal life	Desired it	Needed it
Character	Exemplary	Detested
Response to the Law	Self-righteous	Humbled
Believed (trusted) Jesus	Convicted—but no response	Convicted—whole-hearted response

Repentance towards God and faith in Jesus must be paramount when preaching the gospel. Both sides of the gospel must be preached to those who are seeking eternal life. In order for us to be found, we must first know that we are lost. In order for us to be made righteous, we must first see the judgment for our sin in Jesus. In order for us to receive the grace or unmerited favor of God, we must first see the fruitless merit of our works through the Law. In order for us to have faith in God for our salvation, we must first repent of trying to justify ourselves.

Lost	⇨	Found
Judgment	⇨	Righteousness
Law	⇨	Grace
Repentance	⇨	Faith

Before we share with others the right-hand side of the equation, we must through the Holy Spirit help people to see the left-hand side of the equation. Once people discover themselves in the left-hand side of the equation it will thrust, compel and convict them toward the right. The Word of God and the power of the Holy Spirit enable this to take place.

We err greatly if we share with people the answer before they know the problem. In fact, we will make them twice the child of the devil than they were before.

CHAPTER 4

OUR IDENTITY

In a peaceful suburb, eighteen-month-old Timothy was playing near the fence while his mother went back into the laundry for another load of washing. A woman with a male companion was parked next to the fence. The woman stepped out of the car, picked Timothy up and quietly returned to the car. The vehicle slowly disappeared down the street and out of sight before Timothy's mother returned to the clothesline.

At the clothesline, Timothy's mother bent down and picked up a tiny pair of blue shorts and a couple of pegs. She placed the first peg on the elastic waistline and casually looked over to the fence with a smile in her eyes to see her youngest child. A second glance this time, through a set of sheets, also failed to sight him. She put the other peg on the little waistline and started to wander around the garden to see where he had gone. Curiosity quickly turned to despair and despair to terror, as the search revealed no trace of him. With the yard fully fenced and the gates securely locked, she feared the worst.

JESUS, AUTHOR & FINISHER

She remembered a white car that was parked outside was no longer there. She phoned her husband at work and through sobbing tears she explained the ordeal.

Twelve-and-a-half years of investigations failed to shed any light on the mystery. Then, by what seemed a miracle, Timothy, who had been accustomed to being called Michael, was reunited with his family. Emotions of disbelief, relief and heartache filled each of their lives.

The whole story unfolded over time. Timothy's older brother and sister have both done well in school and have lived exemplary lives. Timothy, on the other hand, has already had numerous run-ins with the police. Nearly every day since he was abducted he had been abused in some way.

His feelings toward his real parents are mixed, wanting to be with them but unsure whether he can live up to the family standards. He feels betrayed that they didn't protect him from being stolen. All his living memories are of abuse and mistreatment. Inside, he feels this is the only kind of life he deserves, for this is who he is. His parents, over the next few years, struggle to see their love and acceptance break through.

In a way similar to this story, our identity has been severely marred, but God, our real Father, has been seeking to find us all the days of our lives because we, also, were abducted at birth. Now, like Timothy, we have been miraculously found and adopted back into our real family, God's family. The Bible says, "He made us accepted in the Beloved" (Ephesians 1:6b).

Our Identity Crisis

Even though we now have a new nature that is created in true righteousness and holiness, we still get confused. Some of the things we do don't fall in line with our new nature. Some of the old habit patterns left behind by our sinful nature come to the foreground. When this happens, we instinctively think that this is who we are, and that we are failing to live up to the Christian

40

standard. Our wrong-doing makes us question our identity—"Are we truly a Christian?"

One scripture that seems to add to this confusion is found in Second Corinthians 5:17—"Therefore, if anyone is in Christ, he is a new creation; old things have passed away; behold all things have become new." Some people think because they still do old things, they must not really be a new creation. This passage can't possibly be talking about our actions and what we do, because there is not a Christian person who has ever lived whose actions were all made new.

A legalistic Christianity would try to suggest that our identity as a new Creation is based solely upon whether our old actions have passed away or not, but this couldn't be further from the truth. The old things that Paul is referring to in the context of Second Corinthians are the aspects of the Old Covenant. Three times in chapter three he refers to the Old Covenant passing away and twice to Jesus taking it away.

Some Christians struggle to believe that they are loved and accepted by God. They get trapped in a performance mentality. When they do something according to their old lifestyle, they question whether God will still love and accept them. They then question their identity and make statements such as, "If I truly was a child of God I wouldn't do such a thing."

We can also read a couple of passages in John's first epistle that may add to condemnation: "Whoever abides in Him does not sin" (1 John 3:6) and "Whoever is born of God does not sin" (1 John 3:9). Again, confusion can reign supreme and we can think if we sin, we must not really have been born of God or must not be abiding in Him. However, John also states at the beginning of his letter, "If anyone sins, we have an Advocate with the Father" (1 John 2:1). What are these scriptures really trying to say to us about sin and our identity?

My wife and I have three wonderful, young children. Each of them at times does things that are wrong. I have said to each of them on occasions, "We are Mulherans and Mulherans don't do such and such." God says the same to us: if we are born of Him, we don't sin. Do you see? Our identity comes from our family and to whom we belong. Our family values define what we do and don't do because of who we are. If we look at it from the reverse perspective, this is where the confusion can come in. These two aspects seem almost identical. Do our actions come from who we are, or do our actions prove who we are? This is where one of the root causes of our identity crisis lies.

If we ever see the need to prove who we are because of what we do, we can be assured that we don't know who we are. Our children each know they are Mulherans because they are born into our family, not because of what they do. They now do certain things because of whom they are, never to prove who they are.

The proof of their identity is in their birth record, not their performance. Even though, as parents, we need to discipline our children for conduct which is not befitting our family values, it is their conduct, not their identity that is in question.

Approval and Performance

Two of the great questions of life are, "Who am I?" and "What am I supposed to do?" The essence of humanity's identity has rested in what it has done. From God's perspective, it is completely the reverse; who we are causes what we do.

God's approval of us doesn't rest upon what we do, but upon who we are, whereas humanity's focus has been to prove who we are by what we do.

God portrayed these aspects clearly at Jesus' baptism. Jesus' ministry life had not commenced before this time, but the Father said, "This is My beloved Son in whom I am well pleased" (Matthew 3:17). The Father announced Jesus' identity and also His approval of Him before He performed any ministry. Jesus knew from His Father who He was and that He was completely accepted. This acceptance wasn't based upon what He had done, but upon who He was.

The devil's great ploy with humanity, especially Christians, is to get them to perform to be approved. If they don't perform, the devil condemns them with the accusation that they aren't really who they are "supposed" to be. By these accusations he sends them into a despairing spiral, thinking that God doesn't accept and approve of them. Therefore they doubt their position as a son or daughter of God.

After Jesus' baptism, the Holy Spirit led Him into the wilderness. There, the devil put forward three temptations to Jesus (the account can be read in Matthew 4:1–10).

Notice the things with which the devil did not tempt Jesus—things that we so often say are temptations. He wasn't tempted with lying, stealing or committing adultery. The essence of His temptation was, "If you are the Son of God." It was Jesus' identity that was being questioned. Satan was essentially saying to Him, "Prove to me that you are the Son of God." Jesus didn't give the slightest notion that He would perform for the devil or that He had any doubt about who He was. He simply responded appropriately with the Word of God to such demands.

These temptations were the root of all temptations.

The devil now tempts us with the same root behind all our temptations. He is saying, "Prove to me that you are a son or daughter of God by resisting this or that. Do you really believe what God has said about you? Do you really know who you are? If you are who God says you are, then show it."

Who Are You? The Identity Issue

Humanity's identity issues commenced in the Garden of Eden. Satan came to Eve and questioned her concerning what God had said about eating of the tree of the knowledge of good and evil.

This is where the devil caused Adam and Eve to doubt what God had already said about them and the tree of the knowledge of good and evil. Right at the outset of creation, it was humanity's identity that was questioned. When it was questioned, they then questioned it themselves. Adam and Eve believed the devil's lie.

He said, "You will not surely die. For God knows that in the day you eat of it your eyes will be opened and you will *be like God*, knowing good and evil" (Genesis 3:4–5 emphasis added).

The devil questioned what they believed about their identity. He questioned whether they really believed and knew that they were like God. Genesis 1:26 states:

Then God said, "Let us make man in Our image, according to our likeness."

Adam and Eve were already like God, for God had made them that way. The devil deceived humanity into having to do something for themselves in order to be like God. That was the first thing the devil ever did to humanity.

Beginning in Genesis and woven throughout the Bible is the thread of questioned identity. From the first Adam's temptation to the second Adam—Jesus— to every other human being, the devil tempts man to question his identity and do something to prove it.

As a Christian, you need to know what God says about you. Jesus recognized and resisted the devil's temptation and went on with His work. Adam and Eve, who were made in the very image of God, fell into the temptation of doing something in order to be like God. As a result, they doubted their identity and relinquished their authority to do what God desired them to do.

Taking Hold of the Word of God

The underlying reason why we fail to understand who we are in Christ (or rather who Christ is in us) rests in our ability to take hold of the Word of God and what God says about us. Jesus was able to resist the testing of His identity because He knew and responded appropriately with the Word of God. The Bible instructs us in who we are and what we are to do. What we do will be the result of knowing who we are. Proverbs 23:7 says, "For as he [a man] thinks in his heart, so is he."

Just before Jesus explained the parable of the sower, He asked two questions: "Do you not understand this parable? How then

44

will you understand all the parables?" (Mark 4:13). To Jesus the parable of the sower was the most important parable of all. If we don't understand this one we will never be able to understand and take hold of the rest. This is the parable of all parables. It is the parable of God sowing His word into our hearts. Jesus was saying if we didn't understand this one, how could we understand any of the others?

We need to understand what takes place when God is trying to get His word into our lives. God's word is "profitable for doctrine, for reproof, for correction, for instruction in righteousness, that the man of God may be complete, thoroughly equipped for every good work" (2 Timothy 3:16–17). Paul exhorted Timothy, "But you must continue in the things which you have learned and been assured of … " (2 Timothy 3:14a).

Learning and being assured of what God says about us is paramount for us to go and do every good work.

Satan Steals the Word

Let's look at Jesus' explanation of the parable. The first situation is when the seed lies on the hard surface of our hearts. The result is Satan comes immediately and takes it away. It is amazing to see what transpires directly after Jesus shares these parables with the disciples. After He shares the last parable, Mark records, "On the same day when evening had come, He said to them, 'Let us cross over to the other side'" (Mark 4:32).

On the very day that Jesus taught the parable of the sower, He spoke the words, "Let us cross over to the other side." Jesus and the disciples entered a boat to cross to the country of the Gadarenes. Jesus took this time to catch up on some sleep, placing His head on a pillow in the stern of the boat. While He was asleep, a great windstorm arose. As the waves filled the boat, the disciples lost sight of Jesus' words: "Let us cross over to the other side." The storm stole the words and left them fearing for their lives.

Jesus and the disciples were poles apart in having confidence in His words. Jesus was so confident that He slept through the storm. The disciples, however, allowed the circumstance to steal Jesus' word out of their hearts. After only a couple of hours, Jesus' teaching was now a vivid reality. Jesus had sown the word; the disciples had allowed it to be stolen immediately.

Not only was the word stolen from their hearts, but Jesus reprimands them for having "no faith." The Bible says, "Faith comes by hearing and hearing by the Word of God" (Romans 10:17). If the devil can steal the Word, he steals our faith. We must not let the devil use any storm or circumstance to steal what the Word of God says about who we are.

Persecution of the Word

The second situation is the rocky ground or ground that has a shallow layer of soil on top of rock. The word is received and begins to grow, but because the soil doesn't have much depth for the roots, it dies. Many people receive a revelation from God's word and share it with others. The people who receive the revelation from God usually have it established deep within themselves. Those who have the revelation shared with them need to work at establishing it deep within their own lives as well.

We return to the Garden of Eden to see a classic example of this situation. In Genesis 2:15, God takes the man and places him in the Garden of Eden to tend and keep it. Then, "the Lord God commanded the man, saying 'of every tree of the garden you may freely eat; but of the tree of the knowledge of good and evil you shall not eat, for in the day that you eat of it you shall surely die'" (Genesis 2:16–17).

To whom did God make this command? The man. It is not until verse twenty-two that Eve is made. The scripture continues, "the serpent was more cunning than any beast of the field" and said to Eve (notice he didn't say to the man), "Has God indeed said, 'You shall not eat of every tree of the garden?'" (Genesis 3:1).

Adam received the revelation directly from God before Eve was created. We are not informed as to how Eve became aware of the command, but most likely Adam relayed it to her. The devil was cunning enough to tempt Eve instead of Adam.

The soil in the stony ground immediately received the Word with gladness, but because it had no root, endured only for a time. "Afterward, when tribulation or persecution arises *for the word's sake*, immediately they stumble" (Mark 4:17 emphasis added).

When we do not have God's word deep within our heart (even a word that others might share with us), we risk it being killed when it is challenged. The devil challenged Eve with, "Has God said." If we have the slightest doubt whether God said something or not, we stand in jeopardy of it being withered away.

We must allow every Word of God to deeply root itself within our lives. As Paul said to Timothy, we must not only learn, but we must also be assured of what God has said. Persecution and challenges will always arise against God's word. The question remains whether our beliefs and assurances of God's word will be deep enough to withstand these challenges.

Killing the Word

The third situation concerned the seed sown among the thorns. Jesus explains these thorns in Mark 4:19.

The cares of this world, the deceitfulness of riches, and the desire of other things entering in choke the word, and it becomes unfruitful.

These are the people who have allowed the Word of God to be established deep within their lives. They know the word and know who they are, but their lives become unfruitful because of other things.

In the Old Testament the Word of God came predominantly through the Prophets. The story of Gehazi, the servant of the Prophet Elisha, is told in Second Kings 5. Gehazi was being groomed as a prophet under the guidance of Elisha. He was constantly around the Word of God.

Naaman, a commander of the Syrian army, had leprosy and came to Elisha to be healed. Elisha instructed him in what to do to be healed. As a result Naaman was made completely whole. Naaman was so grateful he desired to give Elisha a large number of expensive gifts, but Elisha refused his generous offer.

After Naaman had left, Gehazi's heart was consumed with obtaining some of the gifts for himself that his master had refused. He then pursued the entourage and was given two talents of silver and two changes of garments. Upon his return Elisha inquired as to where he had gone. Gehazi vainly tried to deceive him, but Elisha knew exactly what he had done. The final result was the leprosy that was upon Naaman came upon Gehazi.

Imagine the potential that rested upon Gehazi. Elisha was Elijah's servant and received a double portion of his anointing. It is told that Elisha performed twice as many miracles as Elijah. Gehazi could have received a double portion of the double portion. Gehazi had been around the Word of God continually, he knew who he was and what he was to become, but the word in his life was destroyed and became unfruitful.

When we receive the Word of God into our hearts and are firmly established in it, we then need to take heed concerning the cares. These cares try to destroy the fruit we are to bear from the seed we have received.

Take Heed What You Hear

You and I are to live by every word that proceeds from God. Always strive to build God's word deep enough never to be plucked out. Jesus, after explaining the parable of the sower, said: "Take heed what you hear. With the same measure you use, it will be measured to you, and to you who hear, more will be given" (Mark 4:24). This is a great promise to implement in our lives and build upon.

Do you know that you are "accepted in the Beloved?" (Ephesians 1:6), or are you constantly falling into doubt when accused of some failing? Have you allowed those words, "accepted in the Beloved," to course through the innermost chambers of your heart and life with total assurance? Have you mixed this word with such faith that any challenge to it would hopelessly fail?

The devil will always try to challenge your identity. If you are a child of God, he will tempt you to "do this" or "don't do that" to prove who you are. Make sure that your identity is firmly established because you have been born into God's family. It doesn't rest on what you do—it rests on who you are. When you truly know your identity as a son or daughter of God, you won't fall into sin because that is not part of your family's nature or values.

CHAPTER 5

RIGHTLY DIVIDING THE WORD OF TRUTH

In the Canadian Rockies is a stream called Divide Creek. At a point in its course the creek divides around a large boulder. Waters which flow to the left of the boulder rush on into Kicking Horse River and finally into the Pacific Ocean. Waters, which travel to the right, go into the Bow River, which courses into the Saskatchewan River, on into Lake Winnipeg, the Nelson River, Hudson Bay and to the Atlantic Ocean.[7]

Jesus' death and Resurrection is the rock at which the Word of God is clearly divided into the Old and New Covenants. The Old Covenant leads to death, the New Covenant leads to life.

A clear understanding of these Covenants of the Bible is essential if we are to live this wonderful, abundant life Jesus has given us. Men of old were inspired by the Holy Spirit to pen this amazing manual of life. Every passage is profitable for us when we understand it in its context and appropriate application. Confusion, however, can reign when we lack this proper understanding.

Most of the confusion comes from the way we hear different messages being preached or the way we read different verses or chapters in the Bible. It is not necessarily the different messages or the passages of scripture that cause the confusion, but the way in which we assimilate information. The confusion comes from three primary sources:

- not rightly dividing Old Covenant and New Covenant truths
- not rightly comparing spiritual things with spiritual and natural things with natural
- not rightly discerning what part God plays in our lives and what part we play

To obtain a true perspective of scripture and how it relates to us we need to clearly distinguish between these three realms. Confusion takes place when we don't differentiate between each of the respective realms.

I have discovered that if people can rightly divide Old Covenant and New Covenant truths, then the realms of the spiritual and natural, and God's part and our part, become clearer. (To go into detail for each of the realms at this stage, may add to the confusion.) Suffice to say, you should be aware which aspects are relating to which realms when listening to messages or reading the Word.

The Ministries of the Covenants

Some Christians have thought that the Old Covenant relates to us in the same way the New Covenant does. However, the Old Covenant was predominantly a covenant of works to be performed in order to make us right with God. The New Covenant is a covenant of grace, obtaining right relationship with God through what Jesus has done for us, apart from what we could do or deserve.

The ministry of the first Covenant was to bring about death through the letter of the Law and allow that spiritual death to spread to all humanity so God could initiate the second Covenant.

The second Covenant is the ministry of the Spirit, to minister righteousness which leads to life. Paul describes each of the Covenants and how they relate to us as follows:

You are our epistle written in our hearts, known and read by all men; clearly you are an epistle of Christ, ministered by us, written not with ink but by the Spirit of the living God, not on tablets of stone but on tablets of flesh, that is, of the heart. And we have such trust through Christ toward God. Not that we are sufficient of ourselves to think of anything as being from ourselves, but our sufficiency is from God, who also made us sufficient as ministers of the new covenant, not of the letter but of the Spirit; for the letter kills, but the Spirit gives life. But if the ministry of death, written and engraved on stones, was glorious, so that the children of Israel could not look steadily at the face of Moses because of the glory of his countenance, which glory was passing away, how will the ministry of the Spirit not be more glorious? For if the ministry of condemnation had glory, the ministry of righteousness exceeds much more in glory. For even what was made glorious had no glory in this respect, because of the glory that excels (2 Corinthians 3:2–10).

The Old Covenant caused the offense that Adam committed to be passed on to all of humanity. This resulted in all of humanity being condemned before God. It failed to do anything else but show us we were eternally separated from God without hope in this world. Then Jesus appeared as the second Adam, the second figurehead of humanity, and by His one righteous act He caused justification to come upon all those who have been born into His lineage by being "born again." Paul portrays this clearly in the book of Romans by saying:

For if what is passing away was glorious, what remains is much more glorious. Therefore, as through one man's offense judgment came to all men, resulting in condemnation, even so through one Man's righteous act the free gift came to all men, resulting in justification of

53

life. For as by one man's disobedience many were made sinners, so also by one Man's obedience many will be made righteous. Moreover the Law entered that the offense might abound. But where sin abounded, grace abounded much more, so that as sin reigned in death, even so grace might reign through righteousness to eternal life through Jesus Christ our Lord (Romans 5:18–21).

The Purpose of the Old Covenant Law

Throughout the first five books of the Bible, God's law is outlined. One of the best summaries of the Law's purpose is found in Deuteronomy 6:24–25. It says, "And the LORD commanded us to observe all these statutes, to fear the LORD your God, for our good always, that He might preserve us alive, as it is this day. Then it will be for righteousness for us, if we are careful to observe all these commandments before the LORD our God, as He has commanded us."

The whole purpose of the Law was that the people would be righteous before God if they could keep all the commandments. Some Bible scholars who have studied God's Old Covenant law in depth tell us that there are some 613 laws. We are usually only familiar with the Ten Commandments. What is more horrifying than the number of laws, is that none of the Israelites were able to keep all the Law. James says, "For whoever shall keep the whole law, and yet stumble in one point, he is guilty of all" (James 2:10).

For four thousand years, the Jewish people, believed that the only way they could be righteous before God was to keep all His laws. This was a tremendous responsibility that none of them could live up to. God needed to make another way if He was to ever have any righteous people.

Facts about the Law

Following are eleven important facts about the Law:
1. It caused sin to abound all the more: "the law entered that the offense might abound" (Romans 5:20).

2. It couldn't make us perfect or righteous: "for the law made nothing perfect" (Hebrews 7:19a).
3. It is not for the righteous: "knowing this: that the law is not for a righteous person" (1 Timothy 1:9a).
4. It was made for the unrighteous and ungodly: "knowing this: that the law is not for a righteous person but for the lawless and insubordinate, for the ungodly and for sinners, for the unholy and profane, ... and if there is anything contrary to sound doctrine" (1 Timothy 1:9–10b).
5. It gives us the knowledge of sin: "I would not have known sin except through the law" (Romans 7:7b).
6. It makes faith in God void if we are trying to keep it in order to be right with God: "For if those who are of the law are heirs, faith is made void and the promise made of no effect" (Romans 4:14).
7. It brings about the wrath of God. For believers it came upon Jesus, for the unbelievers it will come on the day of judgment: "because the law brings about wrath" (Romans 4:15a).
8. It made the way of salvation possible for all individuals, because through the law God made us all sinners: "For God has committed them all to disobedience, that He might have mercy on all" (Romans 11:32).
9. It made us hopelessly aware of our inadequacy to be righteous on our own in order to bring us to Christ: "the law was our tutor to bring us to Christ, that we might be justified by faith" (Galatians 3:24).
10. It made itself obsolete after it brought us to Christ: "But after faith has come, we are no longer under a tutor" (Galatians 3:25).
11. It causes us to fall from grace if we go back under it in order to be right with God: "You have become estranged from Christ, you who attempt to be justified by law; you have fallen from grace" (Galatians 5:4).

Understanding Law and Grace

When we were born, we inherited a sinful nature. From that moment on, our natural tendency was toward sin. When one of God's commandments was put before us, our natural response was adverse to wholesome behavior. We instinctively saw the alternative. Our sin nature, seeing the alternative, took the opportunity to do wrong because of what the commandment instructed (Romans 7:8). It wasn't that the commandment was bad, it just showed us the alternative. Because of the bias of sin within our lives, our tendency was not toward the good of the commandment but the converse evil, which was revealed.

The commandment that was supposed to bring us life was actually bringing us death (Romans 7:10). Every commandment we are given provides our sinful nature with another opportunity to be active, another opportunity to do what we aren't supposed to do.

God's commandments have never been the problem; it has always been our sinful nature. The commandments just proved that our natural tendency was toward evil and not toward good. Whenever a commandment is put before us, it always gives an opportunity for the flesh to be its sinful self.

Through the Law, we are shown what God desires of us. His law displays the ultimate code of conduct we should show toward Him and others. God still desires us to fulfil these righteous requirements, but keeping us under the Law will never enable this to come to pass. The weakness of our flesh toward sin makes this impossible, hence God designed another way for this to take place (Romans 8:4).

The first thing God needed to do was to abolish the old way. He needed to make the Law, which only enabled and empowered our sinful nature, obsolete. This is where Jesus entered.

When Jesus came, He not only fulfilled the Law, but He also finished the Law when He died on the Cross (Colossians 1:14). Paul said to the Romans, "Therefore, my brethren, you also have become dead to the Law through the body of Christ, that you may be married to another—to Him who was raised from the dead, that you should bear fruit to God. For when we were in the flesh, the sinful passions, which were aroused by the Law, were at work in our members to bear fruit to death. But now we have been delivered from the law, having died to what we were held by, so that we should serve in the newness of the Spirit and not in the oldness of the letter" (Romans 7:4–6).

This new life in the Spirit takes place when we were born again and received our new nature, a nature that is created in "true righteousness and holiness." Our new nature's bias is always toward the things of God. When temptations come, our natural tendency in the spirit is toward good. This is the complete opposite result our flesh had with the Law.

Paul, in his two letters to Timothy, addressed the difference between law and grace. In the first letter, he warned Timothy about those who were teaching the Law. He said that they didn't know what they were talking about. The Law is only "good if one uses it lawfully. Knowing this: that the law is not made for a righteous person, but for the lawless and insubordinate, for the ungodly and for sinners" (1 Timothy 1:8–9).

Instead of instructing Timothy to be strong in the Law, Paul implores him to "be strong in the grace that is in Christ Jesus" (2 Timothy 2:1). The Law was never able to set us free from sin, because of the weakness of our sinful nature. To put a Christian back under the Law will never help him or her do what is right. It will only resurrect the old sinful nature. On the other hand, Paul shows what grace will do when writing to Titus. He said, "the *grace of God* that brings salvation has appeared to all men, teaching us that, denying ungodliness and worldly lusts, we should live soberly, righteously and godly in this present age" (Titus 2:11–12 emphasis added).

A Slave or a Son

John writes, "For the law was given through Moses, but grace and truth came through Jesus Christ" (John 1:17). Moses' law couldn't set us free—it only condemned us and still tries to condemn us. A few chapters later, John quotes Jesus saying, "you shall know the truth and the truth shall make you free" (John 8:32). It is Jesus who makes us free. The Law could never do it.

In this same passage, Jesus illustrates a profound truth about law and grace. He says, "Most assuredly, I say to you, whoever commits sin is a slave of sin. And a slave does not abide in the house forever, but a son abides forever. Therefore if the Son makes you free, you shall be free indeed" (John 8:34–36).

All of humanity has been living in God's house. Before we became Christians, we were slaves under God's law, trying to do what was right, but hopelessly failing to do enough right to be part of His family. Jesus said that only children were qualified to abide in a house forever, not slaves.

Slaves only exist in a household under rules and regulations. They are accepted or rejected solely on their performance: "Have they or have they not measured up to what is required?"

As a slave under God's rules and regulations, we were never able to live up to the standards, hence, we found ourselves banished from His house forever. A child, on the other hand, was accepted in the household solely on the basis of being born into the family.

The Apostle Paul used the same analogy when writing to the Galatians. He said that Jesus came "to redeem those who were under the law, that we might receive adoption as sons ... Therefore you are no longer a slave but a son" (Galatians 4:5,7a).

Under the Dominion of Sin

Just as every part of the earth is under the atmosphere, our old, sinful life was under law. While steeped in the body of sin, we could see, sense and know the heights to which God wanted us to soar, but there was nothing within us to empower us to soar into its heights. We were sin-bound and couldn't break free of its power by anything we did.

The Law's weight, like the heavy atmosphere, pressed on us. The thing that we wanted to soar into only declared how bound to the body of sin we were.

Writing to the Romans, the Apostle Paul, says, "For sin shall not have dominion over you, for you are not under law but under grace" (Romans 6:14). When we go back under the Law, we put ourselves back under the dominion of sin. The Law feeds our old sinful nature and continues to give it opportunity to stay alive. Paul reiterates a similar comment to the Corinthians when he says, "The sting of death is sin, and the strength of sin is the law" (1 Corinthians 15:56).

As long as we stay under the Law's demands, it actually strengthens the very sin from which we desire to be free.

The writer of Hebrew says, "for on the one hand there is an annulling of the former commandments because of its weakness and unprofitability, for the law made nothing perfect; on the other hand, there is a bringing in of a better hope, through which we draw near to God" (Hebrews 7:18–19). The Law was regarded as weak and unprofitable, not because of its essence, but because of its inability to change us.

Is God's Law Sin?

The Apostle Paul says:

Certainly not! On the contrary, I would not have known sin except through the law. For I would not have known covetousness unless the law had said, "You shall not covet." But sin, taking opportunity by the commandment, produced in me all manner of evil desire. For apart from the law sin was dead. I was alive once without the law, but when the commandment came, sin revived and I died. And the commandment, which was to bring life, I found to bring death. For sin, taking occasion by the

59

commandment, deceived me, and by it killed me. Therefore the law is holy, and the commandment holy and just and good (Romans 7b–12).

The Law is holy, just and good.

God is Holy

But as He who called you is holy, you also be holy in all your conduct, because it is written, Be holy, for I am holy (1 Peter 1:15–16).

God is Just

And there is no other God besides Me, a just God and a Savior (Isaiah 45:21).

God is Good

No one is good but One, that is, God (Luke 18:19).

The Law is not sin, it is the very nature and essence of who God is. It is the written expression of His Person, His Righteousness, and His Holiness. It is the written code of His conduct and the indication of His character.

When the Bible says we "put on the new man which was created according to God, in true righteousness and holiness" (Ephesians 4:24), it means we put on the nature of God. We put on His Holiness, His Righteousness, and His Goodness. Out of this new nature we may now fulfil the "righteous requirements of the law" (Romans 8:4). These are the things that our spirit now lives out of, possesses and exists to express. It is no longer duty, or to earn merit; it comes from our heart, the place where God has written it.

The Law, to us, consists no longer of rules; it is relationship. It is the atmosphere and environment within which we are free to dwell and in which we inevitably feel most at home. It is us relating to God through our love for who He is and us relating to others out of love toward them. Love is the fulfillment of the Law.

The Law, to us, no longer consists of regulations; it is our nature.

My eldest brother, Steve, was a wild driver in his younger years. I vividly remember one time when we were going camping with a few of his friends. We were just coming over a rise at Surfers Paradise on the Gold Coast and Steve decided to take the car to its limit. The distance from the top of the rise to a set of traffic lights that had just turned yellow was, in my estimation, nearly half-a-mile away. We made it into the middle of the intersection before the lights had changed to red (you can probably guess we weren't just idling by). We caught a glimpse of the flashing lights of a police car as we passed through the intersection. A fair way down the road, Steve discovered that the lights were still flashing way back in the distance. In an act of good judgment, he decided to pull over and wait for what seemed an eternity for the police car to catch up. I don't know who was more stunned—the policeman, that Steve had actually stopped and waited for him, or Steve, when the policeman let him off with only a warning!

A couple of years later, Steve decided to become a policeman himself and is now an inspector. One day Steve and I were having a conversation about driving habits and speeding. Steve relayed to me the incredible feeling he had shortly after he was made a policeman and, in a sense, had become part of the law. He said, "It's funny; my desire and inclination to speed isn't there any more." Abiding by the law and the speed limit was no longer an issue to him. Not that he was above the law: now he was part of the law.

The Law Was a Shadow

The law was a "shadow of things to come, but the substance is of Christ" (Colossians 2:17).

The Law was a shadow that was cast over us to give us a form to which to conform, but had no substance to transform us. The Law was the empty form that silhouetted the nature and character of God and His Righteousness, but the Law itself, being empty of substance, could never produce in us what God required. Jesus

61

came as the tangible reality and substance of the Law. He was and is Righteousness, Holiness, Goodness and Justice personified.

In union with Jesus Christ (the very body and substance of what the Law depicts), we can now produce the fruits of righteousness and holiness.

In Romans 7, Paul uses a rare illustration to portray a truth concerning freedom from the Law. When I speak of freedom from the Law, I believe that God intended us to be free from an empty form of the Law in order to be able to be married to another, the true substance, Jesus Himself. Paul's illustration depicts a wife being free to marry another, after her husband dies.

While married to, or under the Law, the only fruit that was conceived from our relationship with it was illegitimate, deformed and always resulted in death. In order for God to free us legally from the written law, we needed to die to the Law. God did this for us through the body of Jesus, the whole purpose being, from the new union, fruit would be birthed to God.

Fulfilling Righteous Requirements of the Law

God's aim for both believers and unbelievers has always been to fulfil the righteous requirements of the Law. It has never changed. The reality, however, is that unbelievers cannot. They are held under the Law until the Law either brings about the totality of death or the Holy Spirit brings them to faith in Jesus by convicting them of their sin.

Believers, on the other hand, are able to do what is right through the Holy Spirit. They are freed from the Law and their sinful nature through the death of Jesus in order to fulfil the righteous requirements of the Law.

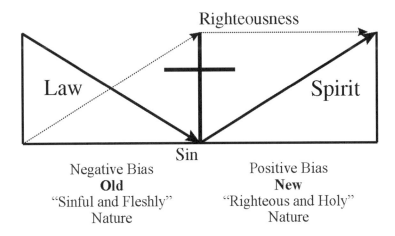

The New Law of Liberty

Samuel Logan Brengle said, "The converted man is bound to his inbred sin, Jesus looses him and he is free indeed. It is a complete deliverance, a perfect liberty, a Heavenly freedom that Jesus gives, by bringing the soul under the law of liberty, which is the law of love."[8]

The Law does not exist now for us in the context of the letter that kills, but in the Spirit, which gives life. What an amazing freedom and relief this gives us—not being concerned with punishment to be avoided, but life's purpose to be fulfilled.

Jesus entered the temple and opened up the book of Isaiah and read:

The Spirit of the LORD is upon Me, Because He has anointed Me To preach the gospel to the poor; He has sent Me to heal the brokenhearted, To proclaim liberty to the captives And recovery of sight to the blind, To set at liberty those who are oppressed (Luke 4:18).

Jesus was anointed not only to proclaim liberty, but also to set the people at liberty. The weight of God's law was too much for the people to bear. The Scribes and Pharisees who were the teachers of the Law only added to the bondage. Jesus, seeing the people struggling under the weight of sin, came to set us free. He said to the people:

> Come to Me, all you who labor and are heavy laden and I will give you rest. Take My yoke upon you and learn of Me, for I am gentle and lowly in heart, and you will find rest for your souls. For My yoke is easy and My burden is light (Matthew 11:28–30).

The liberty that Jesus desires us to enter into is more than a freedom from the guilt and punishment of sin. It is a freedom from death-producing sin itself, the sin that hurts others and hurts God. God's grace and liberty grant us total freedom from both the cause and effects of sin. People who only see God's grace as freedom from the punishment of sin, don't understand the totality of His grace.

The Apostle Paul clarifies this wonderful liberty to the Galatians when he says:

> Stand fast therefore in the liberty by which Christ has made us free, and do not be entangled again with a yoke of bondage" (Galatians 5:1). "For you, brethren, have been called to liberty; only do not use liberty as an opportunity for the flesh, but through love serve one another (Galatians 5:13).

This new law of liberty is the law of love and "against such there is no law" (Galatians 5:23b).

Paul believed that under this new law of liberty that "all things were now lawful for him." Did that mean he could now do anything he wanted? Certainly, but certainly not, he made a clear distinction with regard to three points.

Even though all things were now lawful, he says:
- "But all things are not helpful" (1 Corinthians 6:12).
- "But I will not be brought under the power of any" (1 Corinthians 6:12b).
- "But not all things edify" (1 Corinthians 10:23b).

When we rightly divide the word of truth we obtain a right and true perspective of the Covenants and the Word of God. Paul compelled Timothy to do this, warning him throughout both of his epistles of false and erroneous teaching concerning the Law and other unsound words. When we do likewise we shall not be put to shame because we have studied to show ourselves approved unto God. Paul's beginning plea in Second Timothy 2 was that Timothy would be strong in the grace of God so he might commit this correct teaching to faithful men and others also.

Rightly dividing the word of truth is first for us. When firmly established in us we are able to commit it to others, also. The gospel, although individual, is not private and we have a responsibility to faithfully pass it on to others. I encourage you to diligently study the Word of God, appropriate it to your life, then commit it to others also.

CHAPTER 6

WALKING IN THE SPIRIT

The Christian life, among a host of other things, is about faith and life in the Spirit. Two key scriptures are, "The just shall live by faith" (Romans 1:17b) and "Walk in the Spirit and you shall not fulfil the lusts of the flesh" (Galatians 5:16).

Once a Christian commences his or her spiritual life, the main task is to continue in that faith. Opposition to our walk comes from many different areas, but none more so than from within.

A man once asked D.L. Moody where most of his opposition came from. He replied—"D.L. Moody."

The word "flesh" has a number of meanings in the Bible. In the context of the verse in Galatians, it refers to the carnal nature. The flesh is the part of us that is steeped in corruption. Although the flesh seems to be a strong and powerful force within us, in reality it is dead. Sometimes, however, it tries to resurrect itself. This being the case, we need to discover what the flesh is and how to overcome it.

Some of the thoughts in this chapter I have learned through a tape series by Mike Williams. The Galatians began their Christian lives on the firm foundation of Jesus and Him crucified. Before too long, however, so-called Christian Jews came from Jerusalem adding aspects of the Law for the Galatians to keep in order to be saved. Very quickly, the church at Galatia fell into this deception. It feared that the salvation it had initially attained by faith alone in Jesus was to slip from its grasp if it didn't keep the Law.

The Hindrance of the Flesh

In my fifteen years of pastoring, I have met many Christians (I would say a good majority, myself included) who felt that, after the authoring of their faith, they needed to do or not do certain things in order to "keep saved." This continuous battle to "keep right" with God has preoccupied the thoughts, priorities and efforts of many. Most of their Christian life has been spent trying to keep right with God and hoping to one day be "right enough" to fulfil His plan and purpose for their life.

Paul rebuked the Galatians for beginning in the Spirit, but later trying to be made perfect by the flesh (Galatians 3:3). Picture a farmer who had only ridden horses as his method of transport all his life but is then given a car when his horse dies. Imagine the farmer getting in the car and discovering the speed and comfort of getting from "A" to "B." Then all of a sudden he is reminded of his horse. He gets out of the car, gets back on his horse and starts flogging it to take him the rest of the way. A Christian, after commencing in the Spirit and then trying to perfect his life by the flesh, is like the farmer flogging his dead horse. As ludicrous as this sounds, most of us have done it and, sadly, many Christians are still doing it today.

For what reason do we do this? First, we have knowledge of good and evil, rights and wrongs, "dos" and "don'ts." Second, we think that God expects us to be holy and do what is right. Third, we have a vain imagination that believes we can be "right" on our own.

Through the Law, we know what we should and shouldn't do. We also are correct in thinking that God wants us to do what is right and not what is wrong. However, the Old Covenant, based on law, proved emphatically that no one could do it on his own. This is our fundamental mistake. If, we couldn't overcome sin before we were saved, what makes us think that we can overcome it ourselves after we are saved?

Jesus proved that He alone could resist temptation and overcome sin through His death, burial and Resurrection. As the old hymn clearly reiterates, "What can wash away our sin? Nothing but the blood of Jesus. What can make me whole again? Nothing but the blood of Jesus."

As Christians, we can sometimes fall into the trap of believing we are the masters over our own lives; we are in control. We fail to understand there are two things stronger than man. One is sin, the other is righteousness. Only one of them has mastery over our lives at any time: "For when you were slaves of sin, you were free in regard to righteousness" (Romans 6:20).

How did we become justified before God? Was it by believing in what Jesus had done for us or was it by how well we had lived? The Bible describes the good we had done before we believed as "filthy rags." Only what Jesus has done justifies us before God. It is only through His righteousness that we can stand before the throne of God, cleansed and washed, holy and without spot or wrinkle.

Conflicting Covenants

What purpose then, does the Law (which tells us what is right and wrong) serve? Paul answers this question for us. In Galatians 3:19 he says, "It was added because of transgressions, *till* the Seed should come …" The chapter continues, "the law was our tutor to bring us to Christ, that we might be justified by faith. But after faith has come we are no longer under a tutor" (Galatians 3:24–25 emphasis added).

Through the Law we know what is right and wrong, but we also know there is nothing within ourselves that can enable us to keep it on our own.

The Law couldn't bring mankind back into relationship with God nor give him eternal life, "For if there had been a law given which could have given life, truly righteousness would have been by the law" (Galatians 3:21b). God, therefore, had to establish another way. Paul puts out a challenge to all Christians who want to live by the Law in order to be right before God:

Tell me, you who desire to be under the law, do you not hear the law? For it is written that Abraham had two sons: the one by a bondwoman, the other by a freewoman. But he who was of the bondwoman was born according to the flesh, and he of the freewoman through promise, which things are symbolic. For these are the two covenants: the one from Mount Sinai which gives birth to bondage, which is Hagar; for this Hagar is Mount Sinai in Arabia, and corresponds to Jerusalem which now is, and is in bondage with her children; but the Jerusalem above is free, which is the mother of us all. For it is written: "Rejoice, O barren, You who do not bear! Break forth and shout, You who are not in labor! For the desolate has many more children than she who has a husband." Now we, brethren, as Isaac was, are children of promise. But, as he who was born according to the flesh then persecuted him who was born according to the Spirit, even so it is now. Nevertheless what does the Scripture say? "Cast out the bondwoman and her son, for the son of the bondwoman shall not be heir with the son of the freewoman." So then, brethren, we are not children of the bondwoman but of the free (Galatians 4:21–31).

The two Covenants described here are, first, the Old Covenant which speaks of the Law that leads to bondage and, second, the New Covenant of grace, that leads to freedom and liberty.

Abraham had received a promise from God that he would have a son, a son of promise, through whom the seed would come. Because this promise was taking a long time to manifest itself, Abraham decided to do the work himself. The result was Ishmael.

For a number of years, Ishmael lived as if he were the promise. When Isaac was born by a miracle of God, Abraham and everyone saw him as the promise. Ishmael began to persecute Isaac because he wanted to be part of the blessing and the inheritance. When this happened, both Hagar (the bondwoman—speaking of the Old Covenant, the Law) and Ishmael (her son—speaking of the works or the fruit of the Law) were to be cast out. From that moment there has always been contention between the flesh and the Spirit: "But as he who was born according to the flesh then persecuted him who was born according to the Spirit, even so it is now" (Galatians 4:29). The Apostle Paul goes on to say in Galatians 5:17, "For the flesh lusts against the Spirit and the Spirit against the flesh; and these are contrary to one another, so that you do not do the things that you wish."

Just as Ishmael wanted to be the promise and wanted to be a partaker of the inheritance, our flesh wants to be right with God. It wants what our Spirit has, right relationship with God. It desperately wants to be right and do right, but it can never be right with God, "for by the works of the law no flesh shall be justified" (Galatians 2:16b).

Our flesh nature has two extremities: the desire to be right with God by itself and the desire to be totally depraved. It wants to be both good and evil at the same time. Our flesh nature feeds and lives off the knowledge of good and evil. That is what keeps it alive; that is what keeps it healthy and strong. By continuing to partake of the fruit of the tree of the knowledge of good and evil, our lives continue to live out of the flesh and not the Spirit.

Death of the Flesh

So how do we combat the flesh nature? Galatians 2:20 says, "I have been crucified with Christ; it is no longer I who live, but Christ that lives in me and the life which I now live in the flesh I live by faith in the Son of God who loved me and gave himself for me."

71

When Jesus died on the Cross, a number of things took place. Three of the most profound things that happened are found in Colossians. Paul states "And you, being dead in your trespasses and the uncircumcision of your flesh, He has made alive together with Him, having forgiven you all trespasses, having wiped out the handwriting of requirements that was against us, which was contrary to us. And he has taken it out of the way, having nailed it to the cross" (Colossians 2:13–14).

The requirements the Law identified, to make us right with God, were nailed to the Cross. They were taken out of the way. The Law, which gave us the knowledge of good and evil, has now been consumed by the "Tree of Life." The verses continue: "Having disarmed principalities and powers, He made a public spectacle of them, triumphing over them in it. So let no one judge you in food or in drink, or regarding a festival or a new moon or Sabbaths, which are a shadow of things to come, but the substance is of Christ" (Colossians 2:15–17). Verses 14, 16 and 17 all speak of the Law: therefore, in the context of the Scripture, verse 15 must also be speaking about the Law. Paul is stating that when Jesus disarmed the principalities and powers, He disarmed them of their right to use the Law against us.

Verse 16 confirms this by saying, "So let no one judge you," not even the principalities and powers of your righteousness with God in regard to the Law. Jesus is your righteousness, sanctification and redemption (1 Corinthians 1:30) apart from the Law.

If God has justified you while you were still a sinner, who can bring a charge against you? Who is able to condemn you? If Jesus has justified you knowing all your sin, past, present and future, who can say His blood was not enough? (Romans 8:33–34).

Let's clearly identify these three, powerful truths:
- All our sin that separated us from God has been forgiven.
- The requirements of the Law that we were supposed to live up to, in order to make us right with God, are now obsolete.

- Jesus disarmed the demonic principalities and powers of their right to judge us or condemn us according to the Law.

Feeding the Flesh

Understanding how the flesh works and operates is vital to understanding how to live by the Spirit. Right from the Garden of Eden, the devil's desire has been for humanity to live out of the flesh, to live separated from God, knowing good and evil for itself. The only way humanity can live in the flesh is to live out of the tree of the knowledge of good and evil.

As we mentioned earlier, the flesh wants to live in two ways: first, it wants to be totally depraved, committing sin, and, second, to live self-righteously, making itself right with God. The Law was the old benchmark to tell us what we were doing was either right or wrong in respect to God and to each other. The devil continues to tempt Christians to live in the flesh. His administrative genius tries to put us back under the Law to make us think we need to do this or that to be right with God. If he can convince us of this, he causes us to fall from grace and live in the flesh.

Let me illustrate. As a Christian, you have come to faith in Jesus and you know God is holy and hates sin. Instinctively, your thoughts then tell you to do right to stay right with God. Even though God is holy and hates sin, our motive behind being holy and hating sin must change. The underlying thoughts and motives that tell us to do right and resist sin to keep ourselves right with God are fleshly, sensual and demonic.

You and I can never do anything to be right or keep ourselves right with God other than to have faith in what Jesus has done for us. To do anything apart from faith in Jesus to keep right with God is prideful and self-righteous. Both of these attitudes are paramount within our fleshly, carnal nature.

Does that mean that we shouldn't strive to be holy and resist sin? As Paul says, "Certainly not! How shall we who died to sin live any longer in it?" (Romans 6:2). The flesh desires to be right

73

with God just as much as the Spirit. The great difference, though, lies in motive and ability. The moment you feel you need or want to do something or not do something to be right with God, you are in the flesh. You put yourself back under the works of the Law to be right with God.

Paul said to the Galatians (and would say exactly the same thing to us as a result of this kind of motive), "You have become estranged from Christ, you who attempt to be justified by law; you have fallen from grace" (Galatians 5:4). God's gift of righteousness is not something we deserve, nor is it something we can earn by what we do or don't do. God's righteousness comes to us by grace, through faith alone and not of ourselves.

To walk and live in the Spirit is to walk and live knowing that only in Jesus are we ever in right standing with God. It is not by the works we do for Him, or the sin we resist through Him. Rather, being holy and resisting sin is a fruit of our being right with God through Jesus in the first place.

In Romans 11:6, Paul distinctly clarifies this point. He says, "And if by grace, then it is no longer of works; otherwise grace is no longer grace. But if it is of works, it is no longer grace; otherwise work is no longer work." Being right with God is either through grace or works, but it can't be both. The Law showed us that we couldn't do it through works, however, Jesus showed us that it could only be possible through God's grace.

Grace Enables Life in the Spirit

God's grace never abolishes the necessity of good works; it enables them. Good works never result in right standing with God; they are a fruit of that right relationship.

Under this amazing life in the Spirit, we are free from the pressure to perform to be right with God. In this life of the Spirit, we are set at liberty to soar above the bondage of the Law of sin and death.

During the building of the Golden Gate Bridge over San Francisco Bay, construction fell badly behind schedule because several workers had accidentally fallen from the scaffolding to their deaths. Engineers and administrators could find no solution to the costly delays. Someone suggested a gigantic net be hung under the bridge to catch any who fell.

Finally, in spite of the enormous cost, the engineers opted for the net. After it was installed, progress was hardly interrupted. A worker or two fell into the net but were saved. Ultimately, all the time lost to fear was regained by replacing fear with faith in the net.[9]

The net of God's wonderful grace frees us to live and work for Him all the more and lifts us up again if we fall. "The steps of a good man are ordered by the LORD and He delights in his way. Though he fall, he shall not be utterly cast down. For the Lord upholds him with His hand" (Psalm 37:23–24). This is not a license to sin, but a protection from it.

God's grace can be seen in the same way with a father or mother helping a baby to walk. The father or mother wants to help the baby walk, but knows that it doesn't have the ability in itself. They know the baby will fall initially, so they put safeguards in place so the baby won't hurt itself as it is learning. The mother or father will stay close to catch the baby as it falls. The baby desires to walk, but has some weaknesses and falls from time to time. Even though it doesn't desire to fall and would rather stay upright and walk, the baby still finds itself helplessly falling because of its inadequacies. The parents are there to watch over the baby and protect it so the little one can begin a continuous walk. Without the protection and support of the parents, the baby would find walking extremely difficult to do.

As Christians, we are like that little baby. The only way we will eventually walk right with God is to know the freedom God has given us to venture out with His protection of grace. Grace is the net of liberty that enables us to walk within His reach. Many of us don't venture into the heights to which God desires us to go because we aren't trusting in God's grace to keep us from falling.

We are too concerned with saving our own lives by keeping "safe" within the bounds of the Law, not discerning that we have fallen out of God's grace by doing so. God can't help us while we are trying to do it ourselves.

Sin Consciousness

When we are "sin conscious" rather than "righteousness conscious," we live in the flesh and not the Spirit. The kingdom of God is "righteousness, joy and peace in the Holy Spirit," but so often, as Christians, we are focused on our sin: trying to overcome it, trying to be forgiven for it, trying to resist it, in order to be right with God. We think we need to do all this in order to be in a right position to minister for Him. The trap with this thinking is the more we dwell upon our sin, the more it consumes us. The more consumed we are by our sin, the more we struggle to be free from it and, the more we struggle, the more discouraged we become.

Imagine living a life free from the bounds of sin. What could you dream of doing in God? Paul saw what needed to be done and he was also free to go out and do it. Some of the scars and marks resulting from his ministry are listed in his second letter to the Corinthians. After he listed many things that hindered him and that he also suffered, he makes an amazing statement: "You are not restricted by us, but you are restricted by your own affections" (2 Corinthians 6:12). Paul instructed them not to yoke themselves or commune with sin and the flesh. Being conscious of sin restricts us in what we could do in God.

Hebrews 10 begins by talking about the sacrifices of the Old Testament and how they couldn't make those who approach perfect. Verse two says, "For then would they not have ceased to be offered? For the worshippers, once purified, would have had no more consciousness of sins" (Hebrews 10:2). The chapter goes on to mention Jesus' sacrifice and says, "For by one offering He hath perfected for ever them that are sanctified" (Hebrews 10:14 KJV).

The writer of Hebrews is saying that if the Old Testament sacrifices had done their job and perfected the people, then the people would no longer have been conscious of their sins. Jesus has perfected forever the ones He has sanctified. Therefore, if Jesus' sacrifice has done its job, we should no longer be conscious of our sins because He has totally cleansed us of them. John the Baptist said of Jesus, "Behold! The Lamb of God who takes away the sin of the world!" (John 1:29). The devil wants you conscious of your sin to hold you back and hold you in the flesh so that you will try to make yourself perfect. God, however, wants you to know that He has forgiven you of all your trespasses and taken them away. He wants you to be "righteousness conscious," not "sin conscious" anymore.

Understanding God's Forgiveness

As humans, we sometimes struggle to understand the concept of forgiveness. Let me explain: when someone does something to us, it always resides in our hearts and minds. The old saying, "to forgive and forget," is just not true and it is impossible to do. Whenever we forget something, it is always a passive thing. You don't do anything special to make yourself forget, you just forget. On the other hand, Jeremiah says God "will forgive their iniquity, and their sin I will remember no more" (Jeremiah 31:34). God doesn't forget our sins: He chooses not to remember them any more. Forgetting is passive; "remembering no more" is active and something we choose to do.

Even as God has forgiven you and chosen not to remember your sins, you need to do likewise. To choose not to remember your sins is an act of faith in what God has said and done. This is living in the Spirit; this is the just living by faith. We cannot live this way if we choose to dwell on our sin and see it as having more power over us than Jesus' blood. We place ourselves back in the flesh and under condemnation when this happens. Romans 8:1 says, "There is therefore now no condemnation to those who are in Christ Jesus, who do not walk according to the flesh, but according to the Spirit."

The apostle Paul continues to outline in Romans 8 the keys of walking in the Spirit. He says, "For those who live according the flesh set their minds on the things of the flesh, but those who live according to the Spirit, the things of the Spirit" (Romans 8:5). Now that I have outlined some of the differences between the flesh and the Spirit, it should be easier for you to discern on which one your mind is focused. Having identified this it should now be easier to set your mind on the things of the Spirit and as a result - walk in the Spirit.

CHAPTER 7

THE HOLY SPIRIT'S PURPOSE
IN OUR LIVES

When Jesus was speaking to the disciples concerning the Holy Spirit, He was very clear in outlining the Holy Spirit's function. In this section we are going to look at one specific passage of scripture in John 16. Jesus starts His address with, "Nevertheless I tell you the truth. It is to your advantage that I go away; for if I do not go away, the Helper will not come to you; but if I depart, I will send him to you" (John 16:7).

Can you imagine the disciples when Jesus tells them this? They have just witnessed Lazarus being raised from the dead. They have seen Jesus feed five thousand people with five barley loaves and two small fish. They have been amazed to see a blind man receive his sight. They have seen lepers cleansed and the Scribes and Pharisees confounded by Jesus' words of wisdom. Yet, He has the audacity to say to them, "It is to your advantage that I go away." Can you imagine what the disciples must have been thinking? This is unbelievable. What could be more advantageous than being with you, Jesus?

Yet, Jesus is emphatic that He finish His work and then depart. He knows the gravity of the Comforter's coming. He knows He must complete His mission and depart so the Holy Spirit can commence His vital work in humanity.

Jesus then proceeds to tell the disciples what wonderful works the Holy Spirit will do in our lives.

And when He has come, He will convict the world of sin, and of righteousness, and of judgment: of sin, because they do not believe in Me; of righteousness, because I go to My Father and you see Me no more; of judgment, because the ruler of this world is judged. I still have many things to say to you, but you cannot bear them now. However, when He, the Spirit of truth, has come, He will guide you into all truth; for He will not speak of His own authority, but whatever He hears He will speak; and He will tell you things to come. He will glorify Me, for He will take of what is Mine and declare it to you. All things that the Father has are Mine. Therefore I said that He will take of Mine and declare it to you (John 16:8–15).

From this passage we see that the Holy Spirit's role is to do a number of things:
- bring conviction
- tell us the things Jesus couldn't at the time
- guide us into all truth
- speak to us what He hears Jesus and the Father say
- tell us things to come
- glorify Jesus
- declare to us what belongs to Jesus

Sin

The first stage of the Holy Spirit's work is to convict us "of sin" (John 16:9).

If I were to ask you, as a Christian, "when was the last time you were convicted of sin?" you would most likely respond by saying, "Sometime within the last few days, if not hours." That is the standard response of most Christians, but whom is this portion of scripture really directed towards? "Of sin, because they *do not believe in Me*" (John 16:9 emphasis added).

The Holy Spirit has come to earth to convict people of sin in order to bring them to a belief in Jesus. Convicting people of sin allows them to see they are separated from God and need to turn to Him in order to be saved from sin and its effects. Only when people are convicted of sin do they discover their need of being saved. God doesn't want to condemn people in their sin, He wants to convict them by the Holy Spirit to bring them out of sin and its effects.

The great John Wesley had been preaching for a number of years when someone challenged him concerning his faith. The person asked, "Do you know that you are a child of God?" Wesley couldn't reply. The person continued, "Do you know Jesus Christ?" Wesley deliberated, and then answered, "I know He is the Savior of the world." The person responded, "True, but do you know He has saved you?" Wesley could only answer, "I hope He died to save me."

At that moment, John Wesley was cut to the heart by these words and spent night and day searching the Bible and praying to discover the assurance of his salvation. Finally, at a meeting where Martin Luther's preface to his commentary on Romans was being read, he felt his heart being "strangely warmed." At that point he truly trusted in Jesus. After receiving assurance of his salvation, his ministry took off in tremendous leaps and bounds. His preaching went so far and his message so wide that multitudes came to faith in Jesus, but until he was certain of his own salvation, he couldn't powerfully share the message of salvation with anyone else.

During this first stage the Holy Spirit comes to convict us of sin, because we do not believe in Jesus. The Holy Spirit's task is to take us from a position of unbelief and sin to the place of believing in Jesus and His forgiveness of our sin.

The Holy Spirit wants us to be sure that this part of our lives has been dealt with in order for us to be able to go on. Every one of us has a heart that desires to go on in God, and we can, but we must be sure of what the Word of God is speaking and allow it into our lives. Only when we are sure what God is saying to us can we go on. With this sureness comes a tremendous confidence and boldness to do what God has asked us to do.

You only have to mention the name "John Wesley" and all Christians regard him as one of the mighty men God used in a powerful way, yet, John Wesley was so unsure of his salvation that he had to wrestle with it day and night until he was sure. Only from this point was he able to go out with power and authority to do the work of God. Therefore, the first thing the Holy Spirit does is to convict us of sin in order to bring us to belief in Jesus. This is the foundation of our faith.

Many Christians camp at this point and only allow the Holy Spirit to convict them of sin.

Righteousness

The second stage of the Holy Spirit's work is to convict us "of righteousness, because I go to my Father." Let me ask you another question: When was the last time you were convicted by the Holy Spirit of righteousness? Many would respond, "Have I ever been?" Others might respond, "I have occasionally." But I guarantee that nearly all would say, "The times that I have felt convicted of sin far outweigh the times I have been convicted of righteousness."

Let's bring this into perspective. Who are the ones the Holy Spirit is supposed to convict of sin? Jesus said, those who "do not believe in Me." If you truly trust and believe in Jesus, then the Holy Spirit has already accomplished His first mandate of convicting you of sin. From this point the Holy Spirit wants to progress to the second stage of conviction—convicting you of righteousness. The Bible says, the moment you believe, God imputes righteousness to you (Romans 4:5–6). The Apostle Paul, writing to the Corinthians, says, "For He made Him who knew no sin to be sin for us, that we might become the righteousness of God in Him" (2 Corinthians 5:21). The Apostle Peter states, "who Himself bore our sins in His own body on the tree, that we, having died to sins, might live for righteousness ..." (1 Peter 2:24).

Through the Holy Spirit, God wants to take us from a "sin consciousness" to a "righteousness consciousness." Ephesians 5:8 says, "For you were once darkness, but now you are light in the Lord."

The Holy Spirit desires to let us know who we are. The moment we believe in Jesus, righteousness is imputed to us; therefore, we can come before God. As humans, we can never make ourselves righteous. Only God can do that.

I was trying to illustrate this principle to my children and I said to our eldest son, "Benjamin, this piece of paper here cannot make itself into a plane, can it?" He said, "Of course it can't." I explained to him that with the ability I have, I can fold the paper into a plane and we'd have a lot of fun flying it in the backyard.

The paper can only be something that it is made to be. It doesn't have the ability to become anything it hasn't been made into. The same goes for you and I; we can never be anything we haven't been made to be.

Only after God makes us righteous, through Jesus, can we ever be righteous.

For as by one man's disobedience many were made sinners, so also by one Man's obedience many will be made righteous (Romans 5:19).

As the potter has power over the clay, so God can take us and make us righteous in His sight, and when God decrees something over our lives, it is done. You and I are made righteous. Allow the Holy Spirit to do His proper work in your life by convicting you of it.

The next time you come into the presence of God to pray, know that He has made you righteous. Then pray with the expectation James prayed with: "The effective, fervent prayer of a righteous man avails much" (James 5:16).

Only because of God's righteousness in our lives can we come boldly into His throne of grace.

Let us therefore come boldly to the throne of grace, that we may obtain mercy and find grace to help in time of need (Hebrews 4:16).

What is grace? It is God's unmerited favor, to give you and I whatever we need. God wants to give us everything we need, but when we are wallowing in our sin and condemnation how can we expect to receive anything from God? Whatever is not of faith is sin and only faith receives from God. Allow righteousness to fill you because righteousness is by faith and gives us access to the very throne of God. Let the Holy Spirit convict (prove and convince) you of righteousness.

How much does God really want us to come before Him and inquire of Him? Paul addresses the Romans about God's everlasting love and says, "He who did not spare His own Son, but delivered Him up for us all, how shall He not with Him also freely give us all things?" (Romans 8:32). If God was willing to give His very own Son, He is willing to give us everything else we need. He is going to pour it out, lavishly, on the sons and daughters that He loves so much.

God's righteousness is precious. However, He doesn't just want us to be able to come before His presence to be with Him and receive from Him. He also wants us to know the authority He has regained for us.

Judgment

The third stage of the Holy Spirit's work is to convict us "of judgment, because the ruler of this world is judged" (John 16:11).

As He was saying these words, Jesus knew what He was about to accomplish through His sacrificial death. The judgment of this world and its ruler were about to take place.

"Now is the judgment of this world; now the ruler of this world will be cast out. And I, if I am lifted up from the earth, will draw all peoples to Myself." This He said, signifying by what death He would die (John 12:31–33).

Through His death, Jesus not only paid the penalty of our sin, but also dethroned Satan from his position and authority.

After Jesus had finished His work on the Cross, He went down into Hades (Acts 2:31). There He judged the ruler of this world, the devil. He made a show of him and all the other principalities and powers openly, triumphing over them in it (Colossians 2:15). He made a public spectacle of them. He then took the keys of hell and of death (Revelation 1:18), rose again and said, "All authority has been given to Me in heaven and on earth. Go therefore ..." (Matthew 28:18–19).

The Holy Spirit wants to convict us that the "prince of this world" is judged and that judgment has now been made in our favor. As sons and daughters of God, we originally relinquished our rights to this kingdom on earth through Adam and Eve. Adam and Eve handed over the complete rulership rights of the world to Satan, but Jesus came as the second Adam to take back the right to rule and reign.

The Holy Spirit has come to convict us of this vital truth. Jesus has conquered the devil and has given us all His authority and all His ability over the devil (Luke 10:19). We not only have authority over the devil; we have authority over every single work of the devil. We have authority over every single demon that is in his hoard. We have authority over every single sickness, disease, oppression, depression and possession. We have authority over every single sin, attitude, thought and emotion. We have authority over every one of our resources, possessions and circumstances. All through the mighty name of Jesus.

Allow the Holy Spirit to bring a deep and lasting conviction of these things. Allow Him to take us out of "sin consciousness" to "righteousness consciousness" and from within this "righteousness consciousness" to a prevailing mentality of "conquering consciousness." These convictions of the Holy Spirit are paramount for us to continue Jesus' work in the world. We are to take dominion, subdue the earth, heal the sick, cast out devils and set the captives free. We are to preach the gospel to the poor, heal the broken hearted, proclaim recovery of sight to the blind and set at liberty those who are bruised (Genesis 1:28; Philippians 3:21; Mark 16:17–18; Luke 4:18).

This is what the kingdom of heaven is all about. Jesus has established His rule once more in this earth. He said to the people "the kingdom of heaven is at hand" (Matthew 4:17). He asked the disciples to pray, "Your kingdom come. Your will be done on earth as it is in heaven" (Matthew 6:10). He said to Peter (as a representative of all those who would believe on Him), "And I will give you the keys of the kingdom of heaven, and whatever you bind on earth will be bound in heaven, and whatever you loose on earth will be loosed in heaven" (Matthew 16:19). Finally, He talked about His leaving and giving authority to His servants to continue His work in this sector of His kingdom.

It is like a man going to a far country, who left his house and gave authority to his servants, and to each his work, and commanded the doorkeeper to watch (Mark 13:34).

We must not stay where the devil would try to ensnare us again. He is a liar and tries to keep us bound in whom we were. We need to take the grave clothes off this "quickened spirit" of ours and be all Jesus made us to be. All of creation is waiting to see the manifestation of the sons and daughters of God.

We are set free to rule and reign from our new destiny.

You and I are now seated together in heavenly places with Christ Jesus (Ephesians 2:6), "Far above all principality and power and might and dominion, and every name that is named, not only in this age but also in that which is to come" (Ephesians 1:21). Everything is placed under Jesus' feet, but we are His body and He fills every part of His body completely (Ephesians 1:22–23).

You and I are now made complete in Him: to fulfil our new destiny; to see the Spirit-filled life at work within us; to see the miraculous power of God flowing through us; to see the gospel of salvation speaking through us; to see the delivering power of God setting others free through us; to see the Word of God come alive and at work within us. We are free to see it. We are empowered to do it. We can do it. We will do it. Oh, I pray the Holy Ghost would come upon you now and witness this within your spirit.

Zacharias, who was to be the father of John the Baptist, was burning incense in the temple. All of a sudden the angel Gabriel appeared to him. Zacharias was terrified, but Gabriel quickly tried to calm him down. Gabriel then started to tell him that his prayers had been answered and that he was going to have a son. John would be the forerunner for Jesus. Zacharias questioned Gabriel because he knew his wife was barren. He said, "How can I know that these things will be?"

Gabriel responded, "I am Gabriel, who stands in the presence of God, and was sent to speak to you and bring you these glad tidings. But behold, you will be mute and not able to speak until the day these things take place, because you did not believe my words which will be fulfilled in their own time" (Luke 1:19–20). What power and what authority Gabriel had! We now have that same power to stand in the presence of God and hear what He wants to say to us, because we are righteous. We also now have the authority to go into all the earth and to perform and decree what God is saying.

When we go into the presence of God and hear what He wants us to do, we must come into agreement with Him. We must come into faith with what God says. We must not be like Zacharias who, if he had opportunity, would have negated the words of God before it could be accomplished. This is why I believe he was made mute, "Death and life are in the power of the tongue" (Proverbs 18:21). When we hear a word from God, we are to go and proclaim it. God always confirms His word with signs and wonders following. God's words are never void or empty, but they accomplish what they are sent to perform.

Make sure you spend much time allowing the Holy Spirit to convict you, prove to you and convince you that you are righteous and judgment has been made to your benefit. For far too long, Christians have been bound to thinking that the Holy Spirit's only job was to convict them of sin.

Sin and righteousness can't be mixed. You are righteous; let the Holy Spirit firmly convict you of it. You are righteous not because of what you have done but because Jesus has gone to the Father on your behalf. You are now more than a conqueror, ruling and reigning in Jesus. Let the Holy Spirit firmly convict you of it.

CHAPTER 8

REPENTANCE, RENEWAL AND RESTITUTION

God's amazing grace plays the major part of forming and conforming our lives into the image of Jesus. Throughout the New Testament we find that it is "God who works in you both to will and to do for His good pleasure" (Philippians 2:13). Since God is doing so much within our lives, for which we are eternally grateful, surely we must be expected to play some part as well. But what kind of role do we play in our spiritual formation process?

First, let's recap a couple of points concerning our progress so far. When you first believed you found that it was "by grace you have been saved though faith and that not of yourselves, it is the gift of God, not of works, lest anyone should boast" (Ephesians 2:8–9). Therefore, the total responsibility for your initial believing rested on God alone. Then I pointed out that God's grace sets us free from the Law and the sin it enables. And, third, when we live in the Spirit, the Holy Spirit mortifies the deeds of our flesh.

Since God has performed and is continuing to perform all this good work within us, it is our part to flow with Him. How do we do this practically?

Understanding the Heart

When we became born again we received a new nature; we became a new creation. God creates this new nature within us. The essential characteristics of this new nature are true righteousness and holiness. True righteousness speaks of God's very own righteousness that He gives to us, as opposed to man's own works of righteousness. This new nature is the nature of God Himself.

Even though God's nature is placed within us, our old nature has left sinful habit patterns and strongholds within our lives. This is precisely the place we take on the responsibility of aligning our lives to the new nature God has created within us.

Jesus spoke much concerning the heart, using statements like "It is not what enters a man that defiles him but what proceeds out of his heart" and "every good tree bears good fruit, but a bad tree bears bad fruit" (Matthew 7:17).

Jesus, through His death on the Cross, has laid the axe to the root of the tree of sin that was within our lives and in its place He has put His tree of righteousness and life. Even though this has transpired, you and I still find ourselves committing the very sin we don't want to commit. We have this new nature within us that desires to do right, but often we do wrong. Why is it that we still commit sin?

Most international travellers between the United States and Australia could tell of hair-raising experiences they have had driving on the opposite side of the road. They are so conditioned through habitually driving on one side of the road that it seems unnatural to drive on the other. Furthermore, when there are no visible indicators such as other cars travelling in the right direction, it is easier for the person to unintentionally revert back to the wrong way.

The reason we continue to commit sin after we come to faith in Jesus is that our old nature has been so ingrained in the habit patterns of our heart. The way we have lived in the flesh has been by aligning ourselves with our sin nature. Once we have Jesus' new nature placed within us, we can now realign our lives with it. Many scriptures outline how to do this:

> Put off concerning your former conduct, the old man which grows corrupt according to the deceitful lusts and be renewed in the spirit of your mind, and that you put on the new man which was created according to God in true righteousness and holiness (Ephesians 4:22–24).

> Since you have put off the old man with his deeds and have put on the new man who is renewed in knowledge according to the image of Him who created him (Colossians 3:9–10).

Repentance, a Change of Mind

B.H. Dement in his article on repentance states, "The English word "repent" is derived from the Latin *repoenitere*, and inherits the fault of the Latin, making grief the principal idea and keeping it [the true idea of a change of thought] in the background, if not altogether out of sight—the fundamental New Testament conception of a change of mind with reference to sin."[10] As a result, much of the emphasis on repentance in Christian circles has been placed on two focuses, those of regret/remorse and of changing the way we behave.

Consider people who love the adrenalin rush of driving fast. They are pulled over for speeding on a number of occasions. They pay their hefty fines and lose a few points on their license. They know what they are doing is wrong and need to change their ways. They try to change their driving habits by keeping within the speed limit but, of course, they continually find themselves going back to their old ways. They get frustrated because they fail and can't curb the way they behave. They eventually give up trying because they just can't change that behavior.

Most of us could relate to similar areas within our lives that we have tried or are trying to overcome. The problem with this process is that it doesn't go deep enough. We need to understand that we can never change without previously changing our thinking. As long as a person is a "rev-head" they will never be able to lift their "lead foot."

Repentance is all about a change of mind or change of thinking, which results in a change of behavior. How does a person know when they have repented? Instead of thinking, "I'm not allowed to lie, steal, sleep around or do drugs," we think, "I love being truthful. I love being able to give to others in need."

How does this process work in practice within our lives? Paul addresses the process through two key passages of scripture:

For those who live according to the flesh set their minds on the things of the flesh. But those who live according to the Spirit, the things of the Spirit (Romans 8:5).

For though we walk in the flesh we do not war according to the flesh. For the weapons of our warfare are not carnal but mighty in God for pulling down strongholds, casting down arguments and every high thing that exalts itself against the knowledge of God, bringing every thought into captivity to the obedience of Christ, and being ready to punish all disobedience when your obedience is fulfilled (2 Corinthians 10:3–6).

The first scripture gives us the picture of where Christians and non-Christians live. For the Christians, Paul states, "But you are not in the flesh but in the Spirit, if indeed the Spirit of God dwells in you" (Romans 8:9). Our mind has its root either in the flesh or in the Spirit. As we said in a previous chapter, man has thought he was master over his own life, but there are two things stronger and greater than man. One is sin, the other is righteousness. These are the forces that govern our lives. "But if by the Spirit you put to death the deeds of the body, you will live" (Romans 8:13).

This leads us to the second passage of scripture. How do we work together with the Holy Spirit in order to put to death our sinful deeds? Paul instructs us that we have mighty weapons to pull down sinful strongholds within our lives: we have the precious Holy Spirit who helps us in our weaknesses (Romans

8:26); the sword of the Spirit which is in the Word of God (Ephesians 6:17) and the shield of faith to quench all the fiery darts of the wicked one (Ephesians 6:16) to name a few.

In order to pull down these strongholds of sin within our lives we must know the process of how they are built and established.

A person's heart is the seat of a person's life. The heart is the core of our existence. Out of it flow the issues of life (Proverbs 4:23). Out of its abundance our mouth speaks (Matthew 12:34). As we think within the realm of our heart, so we really are (Proverbs 23:7). God had a plan for you and He declared that He would give you a new heart and put a new spirit within you (Ezekiel 36:26). He also says, "I will put My Spirit within you and cause you to walk in My statutes, and you will keep My judgments and do them … you shall be My people, and I will be your God. I will deliver you from all your uncleannesses" (Ezekiel 36:27–29a).

God has changed the substance and spirit of our heart. The Holy Spirit previously could not work within our heart; He could only work upon our heart to bring us to God. God's laws and commandments were also external forces that could never bring the change our sinful hearts needed, without them being internalized by the Holy Spirit.

At last we are fitted with a new heart and with a new spirit to govern our heart. Now God's Holy Spirit causes us to walk in His ways and delivers us from all the uncleaness that resides within.

Prior to this great transformation within, we had built strongholds of habitual sin, which continue to bear unwanted fruit from our hearts. To destroy the stronghold, we must learn how these strongholds came into being.

How Strongholds Are Formed

Second Corinthians 10:4–5 shows us the process.

A stronghold starts out as a solitary thought which we dwell on. Then we form a picture or imagination about it. We then reason with the thought and weigh its viability against the value or belief system within our heart. Desire is then evoked and we decide which way we will go, either with the thought or against it according to our desire. As time passes and we continue to dwell upon this particular thought pattern, the stronghold is starting to be formed until it is part of us. The stronghold, in abundance, ultimately flows out through our actions both consciously and unconsciously; it becomes part of our nature.

In Old Testament days, most cities were walled and fortified, making them strongholds. There are several accounts of how these strongholds were penetrated or broken down. The hand of God, upon the obedience of the Israelites, supernaturally pushed down the walls of Jericho.

After coming to faith in Jesus many people testify that some old habit patterns of sin simply disappeared, a testimony of God's supernatural power at work within their lives for simple obedience to the gospel.

Another instance was when the Syrians had laid siege to the city of Samaria (2 Kings 6:24). They besieged the whole city until it was in famine. They surrounded it, cutting off all supplies. God supernaturally brings some strongholds to naught within our lives; but others we need to take responsibility for by cutting off supply to them.

I was born again when I was sixteen. At that time, I found myself struggling to keep my thoughts pure. During that year I discovered how not to be conformed to this world, but to be transformed by the renewing of my mind (Romans 12:2). The verse at the end of chapter twelve gave me the key: "Do not be overcome by evil, but overcome evil with good" (Romans 12:21).

I remembered seeing an old war movie, the kind where the army would set up a border checkpoint. There would be a sentry box with guards and a gate. Cars or trucks would be stopped and checked to see if they were carrying friend or foe. I started to do the same thing within my mind, checking thoughts as they came in. I began to tag the wrong thoughts and immediately replace them with good thoughts of what I felt God wanted to build in my life at the time.

Replacing Wrong Strongholds

This set up a two-pronged focus for the strongholds within my heart. First, by stopping the wrong thoughts and refusing to let my mind dwell upon them, I was starving the stronghold that had already been established. I was refusing access to it and depleting its strengths instead of building them further. Second, the new thoughts of godliness were allowing my mind to meditate on things that were true, noble, just, pure, lovely, and of good report (Philippians 4:8). These new thoughts were the seeds to establish new strongholds within my life.

It took about six months of taking the thoughts captive and replacing them with good ones before the two opposing strongholds were reciprocated in magnitude of strength.

I have since discovered a further key of effectiveness in this whole process. If I were to ask you to think of a memory you had ten to fifteen years ago, what would come back to your mind? The vivid thing we can remember gives us a key. The memories we are more apt to recall are nearly always those in which we had strong feelings or emotions associated with them. If I were to ask you to recall a fleeting thought you had years ago, it is very unlikely that you would be able to recall a simple one. Primarily because it wasn't important to you, you didn't feel deeply about it.

A thought is like an impression or a voice we listen to inside our mind. When we take that thought and begin to dwell upon it, it forms a picture or an image in our imagination. An enormous number of athletes use this process to help them become better at their particular sport. This process is effective, but it is not nearly as effective as it could be. Concentrated time is needed for this two-stage process to work and it only lasts as long as we keep up the thought process and meditation.

The third phase to this thought process is found in the heart itself. A person can make a "positive confession" all they like, but it must be accompanied by what the heart feels. Above all else the heart operates on feelings and desire and is the seat of our believing. Jesus said, "He was moved with compassion." When confronted with the knowledge of his impending death, Paul said "But none of these things move me; nor do I count my life dear to myself" (Acts 20:24).

It is when we feel deeply about what we think on that we create a stronghold within our heart. The more we align our thoughts to obey Christ and develop a clear picture and passionate feelings, the more prominent a place the thought takes in our heart.

Once we have this process clearly set, we can begin to pull down the former strongholds and replace them with godly thoughts. I now want to share with you some very important keys to keep the process going until the end.

Jesus Has Bound the Strong Man

Luke 11:21–22 says, "When a strong man, fully armed, guards his own palace, his goods are in peace. But when a stronger man than he comes upon him and overcomes him, he takes from him all his armor in which he trusted and divides his spoils." First, we must know that Jesus has already overcome the strong man of our strongholds.

Second, we must understand that we can't fight spiritual things with our flesh. "The weapons of our warfare are not carnal, but mighty in God for pulling down strongholds" (2 Corinthians 10:4). There are two ways we usually defend ourselves against temptation and both are out of the flesh. First, when a temptation comes to our mind we usually try to defeat it with a thought. More times than not it is a thought like, "I shouldn't do that." We are fighting spirit with flesh in that case. If we are to fight with a thought let it be one from the Word of God, which is the sword of the Spirit. Second, when we try to resist a temptation we immediately do exactly just that, resist the temptation. But God says first submit yourself to Me, then resist the devil and he will flee from you.

Third, we must stand firm in the armor of God and continue to stand until we see the victory. It is during this steadfast standing that we conquer.

After Having Done All, Stand

Finally, my brethren, be strong in the Lord and in the power of His might. Put on the whole armor of God, that you may be able to stand against the wiles of the devil. For we wrestle not against flesh and blood, but against principalities, against powers, against the rulers of the darkness of this age, against spiritual wickedness in the heavenly places. Therefore take up the whole armor of God, that you may be able to withstand in the evil day, and having done all to stand (Ephesians 6:10–13).

For those of you who know this scripture and may have just skipped reading it, please take a few seconds to read it again. In the battle of pulling down strongholds most Christians don't overcome because of this vital step. Picture the following—an army encamped around a stronghold cutting off supplies to it.

What usually happens is we begin trying to cut off supplies to the stronghold by taking the thoughts captive and replacing them with godly ones. But occasionally a temptation associated with the stronghold comes and we give in to it. Having given in once we usually say it doesn't work and then we just give up. But be aware that the stronghold has been there for awhile and has built up many resources, which can keep it active for some time.

Ephesians 6 has two key principles. First, the armor of God is being in Him and not out on your own trying to use carnal, fleshly weapons. Second, after having done all to stand, stand strong in God and stand firm. Every ounce of supplies within the stronghold will eventually be depleted. Never give up. Stand firm and resolute until that happens. It will happen. It just won't happen overnight. You will be amazed as former strongholds of inbred sin are wasted away and at the same time, new godly strongholds are built to perform His will and His good pleasure.

A Clear Conscience Before God and Men

My wife, Vivienne, and I were relaxing one night after our children had gone to bed. Viv was sitting at the table writing a couple of letters and I was lying on the lounge reading a book. We were talking a little as we were both doing our own thing. At some stage, I got up from the lounge and sat down at the table with Viv.

Never in my wildest dreams could I have imagined that such a simple night could change both our lives forever. Our whole married life has been one of great joy and friendship. After ten years, we had developed a deep trust for each other. That night we shared some things that we had never told anyone else ever before. These were things that we had done years before and had plagued us internally until that night.

Previously I could recall that most nights and mornings during my prayer times I would think it necessary to continually ask God for His forgiveness for doing such things, but somehow I had no rest from their insistent reminder.

One of the things I had done was to steal something from a shop. It was a little different compared to the times I had stolen treats as I worked as a small boy in my parents' small grocery business. My four brothers and I saw it as our wages, but Mum and Dad didn't. They would catch us by shutting the little cabinet door against our hand until we let go of our supply.

I went to a large department store to buy a gift for someone, one of those nice, antique looking, dome clocks. I found the section in the shop and noticed the various prices on the different items. Not having much money but wanting to purchase a nice one, I decided on the best clock to buy. When I picked it up I noticed that it had a plastic dome instead of a glass one. Standing right next to it was a glass dome all by itself. In an instant I made the switch, thinking it would look more expensive if it were glass.

I then proceeded to the checkout and paid the price for the item that was supposed to have a plastic dome.

After leaving the shop with my heart still pounding, I was filled with guilt and condemnation. I said to myself, "What have you done?" From that moment I asked God to forgive me but somehow I never "felt" forgiven.

Many years later as I relayed this story to Viv, a weight started to lift from my mind. Taking hold of some of Viv's writing paper, I started to write a letter to the department store telling them what I had done. As a Christian, I asked their forgiveness and enclosed the finance that fully-covered the amount. A few days later I received a letter from them stating that they accepted my letter and that all was forgiven. They further wrote, "We have never had anyone do this before." They didn't know what to do with the money I had sent them other than to return it so I could give it to a charity, which I did.

Now, nearly five years later, I have never had that sin plague me again. I had tried to continually make it right with God, unaware that it was made right with Him the first time. The devil, however, still plagued my conscience because I hadn't made it right with man. I hadn't realized the incredible power of two scriptures, "always strive to have a conscience without offense toward God and men" (Acts 24:16) and "confess your trespasses to one another and pray for one another that you may be healed" (James 5:16). If you have been continually plagued by a sin that you have already made right with God, you probably need to confess it to someone you can trust and make restitution if possible.

No restitution could be made for one of the other sins I confessed to Viv that night. By merely making my conscience right before another, I was free from its bondage from that moment.

It is the most difficult thing in the world to bring into the light a sin that has been hidden in the darkness. Although the darkness may hide it from the view of others, the sin ensnares us within a prison of guilt and condemnation until it is exposed. It is when we walk in God's light and fellowship with each other that the blood of Jesus cleanses us from all sin.

Be like the Apostle Paul and always strive to live with a conscience that is without offense to both God and man. It will be one of the most freeing acts you can ever do. You will be free then to be able to do what God desires instead of being bound to a skeleton that is in your closet.

CHAPTER 9

KEPT BY THE POWER OF GOD

Some years ago on a hot summer day in South Florida, a little boy decided to go for a swim in the old swimming hole behind his house. In a hurry to dive into the cool water, he ran out the back door, leaving behind shoes, socks and shirt as he went. He flew into the water, not realizing that as he swam toward the middle of the lake, an alligator was swimming toward the shore.

His mother—in the house looking out the window—saw the two as they got closer and closer together. In utter fear, she ran toward the water, yelling to her son as loudly as she could. Hearing her voice, the little boy became alarmed and made a U-turn to swim to his mother. It was too late. Just as he reached her, the alligator reached him. From the dock, the mother grabbed her little boy by the arms just as the alligator snatched his legs. That began an incredible tug-of-war between the two. The alligator was much stronger than the mother, but the mother was much too passionate to let go.

A farmer happened to drive by, heard her screams, raced from his truck, took aim and shot the alligator. Remarkably, after weeks and weeks in the hospital, the little boy survived. His legs were

101

extremely scarred by the vicious attack of the animal, and on his arms, were deep scratches where his mother's fingernails dug into his flesh in her effort to hang on to the son she loved.

The newspaper reporter who interviewed the boy after the trauma asked if he would show him his scars. The boy lifted his pant legs. Then, with obvious pride, he said to the reporter, "But look at my arms. I have great scars on my arms, too. I have them because my Mother wouldn't let go."[11]

As long as we live in this world there are dangers that will try to ensnare us, but we have a wonderful God who loves us and desires to keep hold of us.

This story provides a great analogy of our Christian life and the people who are needed in order to keep us. The little boy after being warned of the impending danger submitted to his mother's plea. He turned toward her for her help. As he approached the safety of the jetty he then reached out for her strength. As the mother kept a hold of her son, the farmer hearing the distress of the situation doesn't turn a blind eye, but immediately responded to their need.

The Keeping Process

First, the boy would not have survived if he hadn't heeded the warning of his mother. Second, the boy still needed to reach out to her for her strength. Third, they enlisted the help of another to assist in the situation.

There is some teaching around today that once a person has believed on Jesus his or her eternal destiny is secure, but if it were not possible for a Christian to fall away, why would there be so many warnings in the Bible? My concern is to see every person who comes to faith in Christ also finish in faith. The only way this will take place is if people are kept by the power of God through faith.

I am compelled by God with His jealousy not to lose one. Jesus not only came to seek and save the lost, He also wanted to keep them. He said, "While I was with them in the world, I kept them in Your name. Those whom You gave Me I have kept; and none of them is lost except the son of perdition, that the Scripture might be fulfilled" (John 17:12). If it wasn't possible for someone to be lost after being found, then why did Jesus make this point?

This seems like an awesome responsibility rests on us, that when God gives people to us, we are to keep them in the faith. The truth is primarily, it is God who is praying for and keeping each one.

The individual must also take responsibility for his or her own walk. Paul uses these kinds of statements: "I die daily," "I buffet myself," "I have kept the faith," etc. However, according to the Bible there is another responsibility, found in the first question man ever asked God. The question was, "Am I my brother's keeper?" God didn't answer Cain directly, but He answered it on nearly every subsequent page of the Bible. "Love one another as I have loved you" (John 15:12).

Even though God in His sovereignty is more than able to keep people who come to Him, He has chosen to bring the individual and other Christians around him into the equation as well. When all three are working together, the Bible says, "a threefold cord is not quickly broken" (Ecclesiastes 4:12).

Failure to Keep Ourselves

God had such a passion to save people from their sins that He sent Jesus to die for us. How often do we fail to realize that if He went to that much trouble executing a rescue plan, how much more does He want to keep those whom He has rescued? We tend to abide by the concept that God has saved us, that was His responsibility and now the sole responsibility of keeping that salvation is ours.

We see areas of sin in our lives and ask ourselves, "Why do I struggle with this area?" "How can I beat this thing?" "What could I do to avoid being tempted again?" We then invariably search for the answers to these questions in our actions.

Charles Finney said of Christians who search in this manner, "at one time [they] think they have discovered it in the neglect of one duty; and at another time in the neglect of another. Sometimes they imagine they have found the cause to lie in yielding to one temptation, and sometimes in yielding to another. They put efforts in this direction and that direction, and patch up their righteousness on the one side, while they make a rent in the other side."[12]

We put forth an enormous amount of effort trying to conquer our fleshly failings. We conclude that the reason we sin is because we fail to do a certain duty, which leads us to believe that to eradicate sin we must do our duty to stop committing sin.

Our tendency is to turn to action instead of turning to faith. The Apostle Paul outlined the weakness of our inclination to perform good actions when he said, "For the good that I will to do, I do not do; but the evil I will not to do, that I practice" (Romans 7:19).

Temptations intensify in strength, in proportion to the weakness of our heart (I outlined this as "strongholds" in the last chapter). When we do certain things, we do them because of the strength of the desire, which compels us to action. If we are to conquer sin, the main effort must be directed not on curtailing action but strengthening the heart.

We are told that our hearts are purified by faith (Acts 15:9) and that our faith is the victory that overcomes the world (1 John 5:4). James encourages us to be joyful when trials and temptations come, for it is another opportunity to strengthen faith within our hearts (James 1:2–3). When we are weak in ourselves God can show Himself strong because we are directing our faith toward Him.

If the little boy who was attacked by the alligator wouldn't have believed his mother's cry of impending danger, the end would have resulted in certain death. As Christians we must know that whatever is not of faith is sin. The only way out of sin is to be in faith. Faith is the complete opposite to sin.

God continually warns us of the impending dangers of sin, but it is our belief in Him and what He has said that will determine the right course of action. Faith is the vehicle that begins our deliverance from sin.

When we believe, we heed God's voice and turn to Him for His protection and strength. We can't keep ourselves from sin for it is always stronger than humanity, but when faith fills our heart and we fortify ourselves behind God's shield of faith, all the fiery darts of the enemy are quenched. When faith fills our heart, we resolutely pursue the way of escape that He has provided for us to exit temptation's door.

Continuing in Faith

With the revelation of "justification by faith" alone, Christianity has forged ahead over the last few centuries. It is truths like this that are continuing to be restored to the church, preparing it for Jesus' return. Many church historians warn of not camping at a particular revelation, but urge the church to hold on to new insight and go even further.

The revelation of "justification by faith" has primarily been focused on the initial faith of bringing a person into relationship with Jesus. What an awesome truth this is. We must never lose sight of this, but it is much more than this as well.

Romans 1:17 says, "the just shall live by faith." Justification by faith, then, is not only "the just *beginning* to live by faith," but also the just *continually* living by faith (Romans 1:17) and finally the just being *glorified* by faith. The tragedy in the modern-day church is that so many people have their faith authored, but so many don't seem to finish. The church and its converts have been lulled into a false sense of security in the authority of their faith.

The initial act of believing does not necessarily mean a person will be saved. The devil has claimed too many souls by this false belief. He has led the church to inaction concerning many new believers and lulled new believers into thinking initial belief is all that is required.

Do I believe that Christianity is based on individual merit? God forbid; we are saved by grace through faith alone and that through the merit of Christ. Our task is not to go back to a works mentality for salvation, but to fight the good fight of faith. For without faith (that includes the whole spectrum, authoring, being kept and finishing) it is impossible to please God (Hebrews 11:6). It is not our meritorious works God is after, but our faith in order to keep us by His power.

Much of the New Testament is focused on faith. As Christians we can have total confidence in our security in God, because we are kept by His power in all things. However, being kept by the power of God resides on one premise—our faith. God keeps us in every area of our life but expects us to keep one, that is faith.

Faith is the pivotal point of our lives: by it we are justified, without it we are condemned. No wonder Paul encouraged the church to fight for it.

Paul gives a stern warning to convey a message from the Holy Spirit concerning keeping our faith when he says, "Now the Spirit expressly says that in the latter times some will depart from the faith, giving heed to deceiving spirits and doctrines of demons" (1 Timothy 4:1).

On a number of occasions Paul's passionate warnings were drawn from his own fight of faith. He made statements like, "Not that I have already attained, or am already perfected; but I press on, that I may lay hold of that for which Christ Jesus has also laid hold of me" (Philippians 3:12). Addressing the Corinthians, he said, "But I discipline my body and bring it into subjection, lest, when I have preached to others, I myself should become disqualified" (1 Corinthians 9:27).

One of the final remarks Paul wrote to Timothy was, "I have fought the good fight, I have finished the race, I have kept the faith. Finally, there is laid up for me the crown of righteousness" (2 Timothy 4:7–8).

Paul's whole Christian life was a race to be started and finished. His focus was to get to the end. What was this race all about? First, starting in faith; second, fighting the good fight of faith; and finally, keeping the faith right to the end. That is when the reward is given.

The number one thing Paul instructed through the New Testament was to hold onto faith. For if you have faith in God, you have everything of God and God has everything of you in His hand.

Paul often gave challenges to the Church such as, "Examine yourselves as to whether you are in the faith. Test yourselves. Do you not know yourselves, that Jesus Christ is in you—unless indeed you are disqualified" (2 Corinthians 13:5).

The number one thing that disqualifies Christian lives is their lack of faith. On the other hand, when we have faith we have access to every part of God's grace: His forgiveness of sins, His ability to keep us from sin, all His blessings that pertain both to life and godliness, everything we need. Like Paul we need to do one thing, "Keep the faith."

God declares that He keeps us by His power, but we must keep our faith. Instead of being concerned with 613 laws to keep, we have one—to believe and to continue to believe, for faith works by love, and love is the fulfillment of all the commandments.

You and I have proven emphatically that we can't keep ourselves from sin. That is why we have been crucified with Christ so that it is no longer you and I that live but Christ that lives in us. The life we now live, we live by faith in Jesus (Galatians 2:20). In Jesus, each one of us has been given this measure of faith (Romans 12:3).

When we wanted to do good, we found ourselves doing evil because of our sinful nature, but now we can behold Jesus who was tempted in all points of sin but resisted every one. With our sinful nature now dead and Jesus' new nature and life within us, we can see how sin can be conquered. This is the victory that overcomes the world, even our faith.

We can trust Jesus implicitly to keep us. The Law keeps us in sin's power; God's grace keeps us by His righteous power. These are the only two realms that keep us within their boundaries. When we are in one, we are free from the power of the other.

Keeping the Faith

The Christian Life can be divided into three vital parts:

Authoring of Faith Hebrews 12:2	Kept by Power of God through Faith 1 Peter 1:5	Finishing of Faith Hebrews 12:2
Saved Out of Egypt Exodus	Kept by God in Wilderness Exodus	Promised Land Exodus
Set Free from Sin Romans 6:22	Slaves of God (Righteousness brings Holiness) Romans 6:22	The End, Everlasting Life Romans 6:22
Justified by Faith Romand 5:1	Sanctified—Set Apart by Faith Acts 26:18	Glorified by Faith Romans 5:2
Sin John 16:9	Righteousness John 16:10	Judgment John 16:11

Jude implored us to contend earnestly for the faith, reminding us that "the Lord, having saved the people out of the land of Egypt, afterward destroyed those who did not believe" (Jude 5). The writer of Hebrews reiterated this truth, that the children of Israel didn't mix the Word of God with faith. I believe unbelief is the primary factor in why people who commence in faith fall away somewhere along the road.

Many would be justified in asking, "What if I go back into sin, do I then fall into unbelief?" Or "If at the moment I die, I do not consciously believe, where does that leave me or some of the people I know?"

Mark 11:23 says, "Have faith in God. For assuredly, I say to you whoever says to this mountain, 'Be removed and be cast into the sea,' and does not doubt in his heart, but believes that those things which he says will be done, he will have whatever he says." Jesus here is imploring us to have faith in God. When we think that we will go back into sin or unbelief, what we are doing is doubting God's ability to keep us. The devil always wants us to ask the "what if" questions. A "what if" question is nothing more than a seed of doubt. Inherent within man's nature is the tendency to doubt. However, Jesus says to have faith in God and don't doubt, but believe, then we will receive.

Many times when we approach God in prayer, to keep us from sin or to do something for us, we know that He can do it, but often doubt He will. Instead of doubting God's ability, why not begin to doubt the devil's ability to keep you in sin? You're going to doubt something; why not doubt the one who deserves the doubt? God says, He "is able to keep you from stumbling, and to present you faultless before the presence of His glory with exceeding joy" (Jude 24). So why not believe God and His word which is always true and doubt the devil who has been utterly defeated.

What happens if you do sin? Where does that leave you? The Bible says God has left us with an Advocate, Jesus the Righteous. He doesn't want to condemn you; He wants you to be free.

Writing to the Romans, Paul said, "There is therefore now no condemnation to those who are in Christ Jesus, who do not walk according to the flesh, but according to the Spirit" (Romans 8:1). In this verse Paul talks about a walk. A person's walk is the habitual and deliberate course they freely choose to proceed along. Our character is developed not from one particular act we might perform, but from our walk. Therefore, we need not fear the devil's ploy to lure us back into sin and unbelief. We simply need a habitual and deliberate walk of faith.

God Working in Us

Because the Holy Spirit is the Spirit of life, He cannot do anything other than oppose the flesh and its desires, which inevitably lead to death. When we were born again, it was a work performed by the Holy Spirit so that we had no cause to boast about it ourselves. Paul writes, "we are His workmanship created in Christ Jesus for good works, which God prepared before hand that we should walk in them" (Ephesians 2:10). The preparation for our walk is already complete and suited to a life of good works which flow from His workmanship.

Even though we are to work out our salvation, it is actually God who works in us both to will and to do for His good pleasure (Philippians 2:12–13). If anyone had opportunity to think he could fulfil the Law and do good works on his own it would have been the Apostle Paul. Even he said, "I have no confidence in the flesh." In fact, he counted all his ability to do right on his own as rubbish. Why? That he might be found complete in Jesus' work and not his own. This way God gets the glory not only for authoring our faith, but keeping us through faith and finally finishing our faith.

Paul states in Romans, "That the righteous requirements of the law might be fulfilled in us who do not walk according to the flesh but according to the Spirit" (Romans 8:4). This verse reminds us of our absolute dependency upon God to keep us free from sin and do what He desires. Notice the verse doesn't say that the righteous requirements of the Law are fulfilled *by us*, but rather *in us*. This allows us to see that we don't possess spiritual power we can utilize on our own. Rather, the Holy Spirit is always releasing it through us, but never independent from Himself. This power resides in the Holy Spirit and not in us in whom He dwells.

In Christ

Faith is the door to take you out of yourself and into Jesus.

On the Internet there are what is called "secure sites." These sites are to protect you from adverse and unscrupulous dealings in regards to finances and privacy. When you enter a secured site

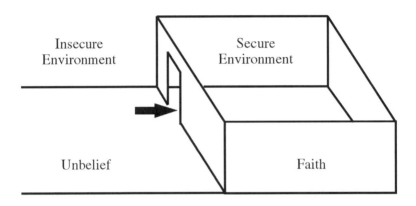

Insecure Environment

Secure Environment

Unbelief

Faith

you pass into an area that is secure from malicious acts toward you. When you go to exit a secured site a warning usually pops up on your screen. The message asks you "do you really want to leave this secure environment?" This warning instructs people of the dangers of being unprotected within the World Wide Web. Jesus has a secure environment for us and it is called faith. When we exit faith we enter the world of sin and unbelief.

In the early days of settling the United States, a group of pioneers seeking a new lifestyle traveled west. In the party were quite a number of families travelling to the new frontier with their horses, wagons and supplies. They had crossed a river some miles back when they were confronted with a life-threatening situation.

On the horizon of the vast, grassy prairie, they could see a thick wall of billowing smoke and flame which stretched as far as the eye could see. The wind was contrary toward them and caused the blaze to devour its way at an enormous pace in their direction. Young children began to panic, fearing for their lives. There was no hope of out-running the fire in either direction or retreating behind the safety of the river.

Thinking quickly, one of the leaders decided to light a fire directly behind them. As the wind blew the new fire back toward the river, there was sufficient time for the embers to cool. They proceeded to move the families, livestock and supplies onto the burnt patch. One young girl, still fearing that the fire would consume her, cried out in terror. A wise gentleman calmed her by saying, "Where the fire has already been, the fire cannot burn again."

At present there is a fire of the judgment of God heading toward humanity and there is no way to outrun it. Two thousand years ago the same fire of the wrath of God was lit upon the sacrifice of Jesus. As we find ourselves in Christ and continue to dwell in Him by faith, the fire of God's wrath won't consume Christ again. All outside of Him will be consumed as the fire burns, but all that are in Him are safe for the fire can't burn there again. What great security we have in Him when we continue to abide in Him by faith.

"But the Lord is faithful, who will establish you and guard you from the evil one" (2 Thessalonians 3:3).

CHAPTER 10

FAITH THAT WORKS BY LOVE

Early Tuesday morning, the eighteenth of April 1995, I woke up to begin my prayer time. I could never have imagined that what would transpire on that fateful day would change my life forever.

Throughout my Christian life there was rarely a moment I didn't feel the presence of God with me. That morning was no different. My first conscious thought as I awoke was of God being so close. It was as if God was sitting beside my bed waiting for me to awake. I greeted Him immediately with a communion from my heart as only the heart can speak without words.

As I stepped out of bed and headed toward the lounge room, we continued our silent communion. Picking up a book by Charles Finney, I began to read an account of someone whom Finney believed had blasphemed the Holy Spirit. My thoughts reflected back to the early days of my Christianity when I had first discovered that dreaded verse and prayed that I would never commit the unpardonable sin.

Closing the book and discarding those thoughts, I began to pray. Everything was perfect. Some twenty minutes transpired and then it happened. In a split second without any warning, I felt like the presence of God left me from my feet up and disappeared into the heavens. Lost for all eternity, I was in total darkness, completely separated from God and devoid of any feeling of His presence.

I immediately felt like a cloak of darkness had been placed over my life. All my thoughts of God's goodness were gone; the words of all the recent Christian choruses, except for a few in the early years I had sung at church, had vanished. The images and pictures of Jesus and the throne room of heaven completely disappeared from my mind. Every positive memory of God was gone. It was as if someone had completely erased the hard drive of a computer.

Thousands of anti-God thoughts and feelings assaulted me. My life was in utter torment; fear filled every morsel of my being. I was nearly going insane with the reality of being lost forever. I had committed the unpardonable sin and was doomed to spend eternity in hell—that was the only plausible explanation.

Trying to reassure myself, I thought, "But I didn't say anything blasphemous about the Holy Spirit; I was in the middle of my prayer time." Deceptive thoughts counter-attacked by saying, "it was a delayed reaction of something I said some time ago."

Continuing in prayer I tried to thwart this attack of the devil to seemingly no avail. For four years I battled this continuing assault of thousands upon thousands of anti-God thoughts and feelings every single day. During the fifth year the fruit of the battle was finally evident with most of the negative thoughts now gone, but still no tangible presence of God. I was hanging only to the hope that someday I would come through this totally and have the fullness of my salvation restored. My best friend, my wife, Viv, was my lifeline; I could never have made it without her. She was my encouragement, my support and my inspiration.

Six years have passed and my life is all but completely restored to the place it was before that fateful day. I have no answers as to why this happened. Yet, if it were only to help the people who came to me during this time with very similar experiences, I would (hesitantly) go through it all again, just for them.

The only thoughts that occupied my mind in the early stages were to "regain my salvation." I was preoccupied with "seeking to save my own life."

I remember reading a book by Brother Lawrence called *The Practice of the Presence of God*. He stated that the worst possible trial he thought anyone could go through would be to lose the presence of God. When I read that statement I said within myself, "You're not wrong, Brother Lawrence!"

A number of days later I received word that the child of a couple whom I knew had just committed suicide. This jolted me back into reality. I came to realize that there was something worse than losing the presence of God, it was to lose your children without them being saved.

Love Seeks Not Its Own

This whole experience revealed to me just how self-centered I was. For the majority of those first four years, my attention was directed toward "regaining my salvation" and God's presence. Although as a pastor I still fulfilled my duties with hardly a soul knowing what I was going through, my internal focus was primarily on myself. I was consumed with my survival, striving to do everything to bring myself back into right relationship with God. I didn't understand that the more I strove in my own flesh, the further I was putting God out of reach.

Many people have never and will never (thank God) go through an ordeal like that. But for many, the internal struggles to keep them saved or in right relationship with God still occupy a substantial portion of their focus. Imagine if we were secure enough in God's love for us that we could release all the love that we so often direct toward ourselves and give it back to others.

Jesus said, "For whoever desires to save his life will lose it, but whoever loses his life for My sake will save it" (Luke 9:24). Paul writes, "love ... seeks not its own" (1 Corinthians 13:5).

Oh, that we would see and live the truth that is evident within these statements! When we put our faith in God to keep us (as we learned in the last chapter), we can then be released from ourselves to others. Paul and Moses both made statements like, "For I wish that I myself were accursed from Christ for my brethren" (Romans 9:3). Their focus was quite markedly not upon themselves, but on others.

Through my time of trial and testing, God showed me many powerful truths. In the midst of the storm, He gave me four anchors to hold me. The first came the following day at our Wednesday night home group meeting. Viv told everyone I was going through something but didn't elaborate on the details; she simply asked them to pray for me.

I didn't hear anyone praying except Darren Trinder, who was standing right in front of me. He prayed, "God restore to him everything that has been stolen from his life." Darren could never have imagined what strength his words gave me. God was letting me know that it was an attack after all and that everything would be restored.

A second anchor came nineteen months later during our International Conference. Amid some 2,500 people, a prophet who was one of the keynote speakers said, "I have a word from God for a Brian Mul... something." He prophesied, "You have weathered the storm and you have weathered the seas and because you have not let go of Me, I am not letting go of you, says the Lord. And I'm going to restore and I'm going to renew and I've still got a work yet for you to do." You could imagine the hope that filled my heart. It was another anchor to hold me steady through this storm.

Nine months more passed. Still in unbearable torment and through sobbing tears I cried out to God and said, "I can't take this any longer, Father." God's response was quick and with words so clear it was almost audible. He said, "Psalm 109:2–3." I quickly opened my Bible and read:

> For the mouth of the wicked and the mouth of the deceitful have opened against me with a lying tongue. They have also surrounded me with words of hatred, and fought against me without a cause. In return for my love they are my accusers, but I give myself to prayer. Thus they have rewarded me evil for good and hatred for my love."

The final anchor came while studying the trial of Job. I came to the understanding that like Job, something I had greatly feared had come upon me. Not that I had committed the unpardonable sin, but I received the seeming consequences as if I had. I thank God that I have a wife like mine and not like Job's who encouraged him to do the opposite of what Viv did for me.

After reading nearly the complete book of Job, I came to the verse of Job's deliverance. "And the Lord restored Job's losses *when he prayed for his friends.* Indeed *the Lord gave Job twice as much as he had before*" (Job 42:10 emphasis added). When Job was able to take his focus off himself and turn it to others, God was then able to move on Job's behalf. As long as Job was trying to solve his own problem, God couldn't move toward him.

God's principles are still the same today. When love doesn't seek its own, it allows faith to operate powerfully from within our lives. When our focus is on God and others we become a vessel for faith and love to flow, not a dam for it to be harbored and become stagnate. Our faith works through love.

True Faith and Love Are Inseparable

Faith and love in the Christian life are inseparable. Neither can operate effectively without the other. It is possible to have faith which can remove mountains. But without love that is not the faith God requires from us. He requires a faith that works through and because of love.

When we have faith in how much God loves us, then we are free from trying to keep our own salvation and we begin to reach out to others. This is what Christianity is all about. If we are to progress beyond the status quo of mediocre Christianity, God's love must grow to consume our lives.

Initially, God's love enabled faith to come to our lives. That faith in turn shed the love of the Father abroad in our hearts by the Holy Spirit. Faith and love are then to continue cycling in our lives to produce and work through each other.

At this point let me ask you a question: How far has the love of the Father been shed abroad in your heart? How far has it consumed the love for self and the love of the world?

We must see that these two virtues are commodities of the heart and that the heart is purified by both of them. Paul says our heart is purified by faith (Acts 15:9). Peter says it is also purified by love. He said, "Since you have purified your souls in obeying the truth through the Spirit in sincere love of the brethren, love one another fervently with a pure heart" (1 Peter 1:22).

The true nature and measurement of our faith resides in the true nature and measurement of love that resides in our heart. Look into your heart to where faith and love reside. What kind of love abides there and where is it directed? If it is to gain for yourself, then you lose. If it is for the gain of another, then you can't lose.

Many people in the world are seeking success. Many Christians are also seeking success. But what is the success we are aiming for? God has the only foolproof plan. You can be a total success if you follow His three-word rule. Can you imagine never failing but always succeeding? Then dwell on His statement: "Love never fails."

The most successful person in the world isn't the richest or the cleverest, but the person who operates out of God's kind of love. You can never lose by laying down your life for another. You can never lose by sacrificing your time, energy or finances for another, as long as you do it out of love. This isn't a love that desires something in return, but a love that abandons itself for the benefit of another. This is the type of mature love that God desires to perfect in us. Jesus said when we love each other with this type of love, then the world would know we are His disciples.

Unconditional Love

Generally, the world relates out of a conditional love. "If you do this, I will do that." People usually think about themselves before thinking about others. Before committing to something or someone, the internal question is: "What's in it for me?" This type of love is the love of the world.

"Do not love the world or the things in the world. If anyone loves the world, the love of the Father is not in Him. For all that is in the world—the lust of the flesh, the lust of the eyes and the pride of life—is not of the Father but is of the world. And the world is passing away and the lust of it" (1 John 2:15–17).

John clarifies that the world's type of love is really lust: things that gratify the flesh, things that our eyes desire and the pride of life. Lust always thinks about what's in it for me, before any thought for anyone else. Lust is predominantly about taking and sometimes disguised with a little bit of giving.

This conditional love of the world is in complete contrast to the unconditional love of God. The world's love is a selfish exchange, seeking the best for itself. God's love is a selfless exchange seeking the best for others. When we consider ourselves in the equation of love, we automatically evoke the world's love. God's love is evoked when we wholeheartedly consider the recipient.

It is startling to wake up to the reality of what we receive from each type of love. Love that seeks to obtain is always disappointed; love that seeks to cause gain is always rewarded. The famous words of Francis of Assisi promote this truth: "It is in giving that we receive."

In God's economy, we only get to keep what we selflessly give away. Jesus said, "For whoever desires to save his life will lose it, but whoever loses his life for My sake will find it" (Matthew 16:25). The things that we are so desperate to obtain are only received by giving them selflessly away. Our worldly economy is the complete opposite to God's and yet we so often trade our lives in its false commodity.

Unconditional love is the most costly love that anyone could afford. There is no price higher than to trade in its economy, for it will cost you your life. The rewards, however, are out of this world. Not only will you receive your life in all its fullness, but you will also receive the treasures for its investments.

Jesus' unconditional love cost Him everything: He emptied Himself of all His godly glory, suffered the total wrath of God for our sins and was smitten. He not only received His life back, but also inherited heaven again and those who would believe on Him out of the world.

John Powell, S.J., in his book *Unconditional Love*, explains very clearly the cost of unconditional love. He says, "Every commitment is like every moment of life; there is a birth and a death in every moment. Something is and something else can never be again. There is a choice and a surrender, a 'yes' and a 'no.'"[13]

When Viv and I fell in love and chose to marry each other we made an unconditional commitment to each other. At the moment we were pronounced husband and wife there was a birth and a death, a choice and a surrender and a yes and a no. There was a birth of our wonderful life together and a death not only to our individual lives, but also to all other possible companions for us. There was a 'yes' to each other and a 'no' to everyone else.

We truly have had one of those dream marriages. If I were to spend my whole life trying to get what I have received from Viv, it would be impossible. Viv has given more into my life than I could ever have asked for or acquired by my own hand.

God has designed each of us this way. Neither marriage nor any other love relationship is ever a 50%–50% partnership. It should always be 100%–100%. If I give 100% to Viv and she gives 100% to me, we never lack and are always totally fulfilled. It is when we keep 50% for ourselves and only give 50% away that we come into lack.

Jesus gave us a commission, "Go therefore and make disciples" (Matthew 28:19). Why did He make such a statement? I believe it was primarily because we cannot "make" ourselves. God has uniquely gifted each of us to benefit one another and to cause increase in the body. It is only when we withhold what we have that we tend towards poverty and cause lack in others as well.

Loving God and others unconditionally will always produce both life and death: Life to others and death to self. Jesus, being very God and very man, said about Himself, "The Son of Man did not come to be served, but to serve and to give His life a ransom for many" (Matthew 20:28). Jesus had every right to be served by His creation as God, but chose to serve and die. In serving and dying Jesus proved emphatically His very nature and essence as God and gave an example of how to truly live in a godly manner.

A love that chooses to serve and die for another is birthed out of the heart and nature of God.

Jesus' life of faith always worked by love—His love for the Father and His love for us. The miracles He performed by faith were never on demand to prove who He was; they were always because He loved people. Jesus never performed a miracle with the thought of proving who He was. He was always moved with compassion and faith. Every time Jesus operated in faith it was always out of love.

How often do we find ourselves doing something for God or others with the main focus on us receiving a reward or recognition? Love does not seek its own. Jesus said, "But seek first the kingdom of God and His righteousness and all these things shall be added to you" (Matthew 6:33). God's kingdom is all about loving Him and others. When we do this, everything we need is totally provided for through Him.

The Law of Love

When God gave His law to Moses, it outlined the conduct we should have toward Him and others. In fact, the Ten Commandments were on two tables of stone: the first predominantly outlined what to do in order to love God; the second outlined what was required to love one another.

The Law, which was given to Moses, ultimately brought us into bondage and produced death because of the weakness of our flesh. It only enabled us to do the exact opposite because of the opportunity it gave to our sinful nature.

Seeing what the Law couldn't do, God sent Jesus to fulfil the Law and set us at liberty. Jesus' love for God and us totally fulfilled every one of the commandments. For love is the fulfillment of the Law.

This liberty from liability has freed us to serve one another through love (Galatians 5:13). Now as we are led by the Holy Spirit we are not under the old law which gave opportunity for the flesh to commit adultery, uncleanness, hatred, murder etc. (Galatians 5:18–21). We are released to live in the Spirit whose fruit "is love, joy, peace ... Against such there is no law" (Galatians 5:22–23).

We no longer do things (or not do things) because of rules or regulations or rights and wrongs. We are now able to do and not do because of love for God and for each other. This frees us from binding obligations and releases us to minister out of relationship with others. When we do something because of rules and regulations, we always do it for ourselves as protection from the consequences. When we do something out of love, we always do it for the one we love. This is the ultimate distinction between the Law that was given by Moses and the grace and truth that was given by Jesus.

A Faith that Works

In reality love is greater than faith and true faith operates through and because of this love. Paul says, "And now abide faith, hope, love, these three; but the greatest of these is love" (1 Corinthians 13:13). True faith believes because love believes all things. True faith endures because love endures all things. True faith is the substance of things hoped for because love hopes all things. Apart from love, faith is nothing. Because of love, faith can be everything.

When we have a love that believes all things, we will have a faith that believes all things. When we have a love that endures all things, we will have a faith that endures all things. This is how the true nature of faith operates within our lives.

Faith operates from the motive and heart of love. To win souls to Christ for any other reason than because we love them accrues nothing to our account. To give everything we have to someone who is needy in order to benefit our relationship with God will do nothing for us other than make us the poor one.

Throughout this book I have shared much about faith being one of the primary ingredients of the Christian life, but I would be totally amiss not to place it in its proper perspective once the foundation has been laid. Paul and James both clearly define the type of faith I have outlined in this chapter.

Paul, writing to the Corinthians, states, "though I have all faith, so that I could remove mountains, but have not love, I am nothing" (1 Corinthians 13:2). James instructs, "If a brother or sister is naked and destitute of daily food, and one of you says to them, 'Depart in peace, be warmed and filled,' but you do not give them the things which are needed for the body, what does it profit? Thus also faith by itself, if it does not have works, is dead" (James 2:15–17). James goes on to mention that demons have faith, but are completely devoid of a faith that profits them or others.

What type of faith is the gospel based upon? Paul declares it is neither about works, which produce faith, nor faith and works, but a faith, which works.

- Works for faith   Galatians 2:16
- Faith and works   Galatians 3:23
- Faith which works   Galatians 5:6

Our faith, once established, is a faith that works. The more filled with love, the more effectual our faith will be in ministering to others. Never allow the faith and love God has put within our hearts to be directed toward us alone. We have been purchased with a price. God has secured us, now let us go and allow Him to secure others through us.

CHAPTER 11

LIVING UNDER GOD'S GRACE

One afternoon, I took my children home from school so my wife could go shopping. As we hopped out of the car, I asked our littlest boy, Matthew, to get the mail from the letterbox. There was only one letter addressed to my wife, Viv. It was a familiar looking envelope from the government, the type that informed her of the family payments she would receive.

As most normal, inquisitive husbands would do, I opened the mail expecting to see an increase in the payment. However, when I opened it, I read the new schedule of payments for the month of May. Instead of progressing up, they progressed down. My attitude was one of, "Why are they decreasing the payment?"

If anything, the payment, in my opinion, should have been going up. I thought to myself, "Why would they be doing this to us when we were entitled to the money we had previously been receiving?" We had not sent them any information of a pay increase or anything that would have, in my opinion, warranted the decrease.

For a good few minutes I was quite upset, thinking I should write them a letter. As with most males, I had jumped to a conclusion without having read the whole letter. Down at the bottom of the letter there was a caption, which was written in bold, highlighted, large, capital letters. It read: IMPORTANT INFORMATION. The following line read, "We cannot pay you as much Family Tax Benefit Part B because you have no dependent children under five."

When I read that line, I started to get more heated. My thoughts declared, "What do you mean we don't have any children under five?" Our son, Matthew, was four at the time (take into consideration that the letter was sent at the end of April). I hadn't realized how close the eighth of May, Matthew's birthday, was. It still didn't register until I read the break up of the progress payments at the start of the letter. The first payment was as normal. The second payment, in which Matthew's birthday fell in the middle, was slightly less. Then the third payment, which was the fortnight after, indicated the amount we would receive from that date on.

It wasn't until I read this that it finally registered. My heart sank within me when I realized they were completely right, even to the last cent. The government was being extremely thoughtful in advising us that in a couple of weeks we wouldn't be receiving as much benefit as before.

Each year millions of Australians receive amazing assistance from the government. To my shame, I saw the payment as our right, what we were entitled to, not as a privilege. Instead of being grateful and appreciative of what we received, I grumbled and complained over a minor decrease.

Shortly after this incident I read a book by Jerry Bridges called *Transforming Grace*, which radically changed my outlook on life. Many of the thoughts in this chapter have been inspired by his wonderful view of God's grace.

I thought, "Imagine what life would be like if I always lived life from the perspective of God's wonderful grace?" I began to imagine that everything I received was neither deserved nor earned. Life was now becoming a realm in which Christmas could take place every moment of the day, not with respect to exchanging gifts (as we tend to do), but with independent acts of giving and receiving. I began to thank God for things I took for granted. A whole new set of thankful and grateful responses toward life began to emerge.

Our attitudes and responses shape our lives. Both of these attributes are powerful forces that govern our whole being in relationship to God and others. Imagine what life would be like for you if you always lived out of a grateful heart. Imagine the impact you would have on your family and friends. Imagine the impact in your church and community.

Responding to God's Grace

A rich young ruler had come to Jesus seeking what he needed to do to inherit eternal life. He was told to "go sell what you have and give to the poor and you will have treasure in heaven; and come, follow Me" (Matthew 19:21). Jesus then explained how hard it was for a rich man to enter the kingdom of heaven. The disciples were absolutely astonished at His example of a camel (the largest animal in their region) going through the eye of a needle (the smallest opening they could imagine). Seeing the enormity of the problem, they asked the bewildering question, "Who then can be saved?"

Jesus explained to them that salvation is something that is impossible for us to achieve, and only through God is it possible at all. Peter was probably relieved by Jesus' answer, taking into consideration what Jesus had asked the rich young ruler to do. He proceeded to ask Jesus with a somewhat blatant tenacity, "We have left all and followed You. Therefore what shall we have?" (Matthew 19:27).

Peter and the other disciples had an attitude of "What are we entitled to; what reward will we receive for what we have done for you, Jesus?" Jesus then proceeded to tell them a parable concerning the kingdom of heaven. Jesus said:

For the kingdom of heaven is like a landowner who went out early in the morning to hire laborers for his vineyard. Now when he had agreed with the laborers for a denarius a day, he sent them into his vineyard. And he went out about the third hour and saw others standing idle in the marketplace, and said to them, "You also go into the vineyard, and whatever is right I will give you." So they went. Again he went out about the sixth and the ninth hour, and did likewise. And about the eleventh hour he went out and found others standing idle, and said to them, "Why have you been standing here idle all day?" They said to him, "Because no one hired us." He said to them, "You also go into the vineyard, and whatever is right you will receive." So when evening had come, the owner of the vineyard said to his steward, "Call the laborers and give them their wages, beginning with the last to the first." And when those came who were hired about the eleventh hour, they each received a denarius. But when the first came, they supposed that they would receive more; and they likewise received each a denarius. And when they had received it, they complained against the landowner, saying, "These last men have worked only one hour, and you made them equal to us who have borne the burden and the heat of the day." But he answered one of them and said, "Friend, I am doing you no wrong. Did you not agree with me for a denarius? Take what is yours and go your way. I wish to give to this last man the same as to you. Is it not lawful for me to do what I wish with my own things? Or is your eye evil because I am good?" So the last will be first, and the first last. For many are called, but few chosen (Matthew 20:1–16).

There are three, distinctly different responses that we can draw from the workers in this parable. Each group responded to the landowner in different ways.

People Who See the Landowner as Unfair

Many people after reading this parable see the landowner as very unfair. Even as Christians, knowing that the landowner is supposed to represent God, most find it difficult to see the landowner as fair. The injustice lies in seeing those who have worked twelve hours receive exactly the same pay as those who have worked for only one hour. This seems grossly unjust. Startling as it may seem, this gross injustice is only seen from one perspective, when we see ourselves in the position of the twelve-hour workers.

Jerry Bridges writes, "Christians instinctively identify with the workers who had worked all day. We place ourselves in their shoes instead of in the shoes of those who worked only one hour. We consider ourselves to be twelve-hour workers, and we expect to be rewarded accordingly."[14]

Imagine you are actually in the position of one of the twelve-hour workers. What would you think?

You have worked hard the whole day, right through all the heat and the pain. At various times during the day you see the other workers come and start to help out. In your heart you are so grateful they have come to lighten the workload. You get to the end of the day exhausted, ready to receive your wage. Then you see the ones who have worked only one hour get called up to receive their pay first. You see them receive a hundred dollars for their work. Initially, you are stunned to see them get that much, but then you think to yourself, "Wow! If the landowner has given them that much for one hour of work, then surely he is going to give us twelve times as much." The thought of $1,200 would have your mind racing, "I could buy this and I could buy that."

It is then your turn to receive your wages. Imagine the horror and utter devastation you feel when you receive exactly the same amount as the one-hour workers. You feel totally ripped off. "How could that guy only give me that much for all I've done for him? He is so unfair, completely unjust."

When we place ourselves in this position we subject ourselves to the following attitudes:

- We have an attitude that God owes us something.
- We think we deserve more for the duty we perform.
- We place ourselves in a position of self-righteousness.

What are the results of this type of thinking?

- The more we think we have earned—the more we think God is unjust.
- The more we think we deserve—the more ungrateful we become for what we do receive.

Jerry Bridges goes on to give a classic illustration addressing the absurdity of thinking we deserve anything from God for what we do. He says:

Suppose you perfectly obeyed all the traffic laws in your state. You always stay within the speed limit, always come to a complete stop at stop signs, always drive in the proper lane, always use your turning signals—always obeyed every traffic rule. Do you receive any reward? Not at all, that's what you are supposed to do. You have only done your duty. You do not, by your perfect obedience of the traffic laws, obligate the state to reward you in any manner. All you can say is, "I have only done my duty."[15]

How many times in our lives have we thought we deserved to be rewarded by God for obeying His laws? And yet we have not even come close to fulfilling His minimum requirement, which is to obey all of them. How distorted a view has humanity had of itself and God? But, when we see God from the proper perspective we see how gracious He really is toward us in our pretentious state.

We live in such a self-oriented world that we lose sight of God and others. Imagine losing this sense of entitlement and deserving. How free would we become in simply focusing on God and others. How grateful would we become for the things we receive? How gracious would we become to others as God has been toward us?

Our self-righteous attitude of thinking that we deserve from God has caused us to lose sight of the blessings we receive every moment. Not only does this attitude affect how we relate to God, but also how we relate to each other. Often we can have the attitude that someone owes us something because of what we have done for them. I use one of Paul's statements to describe this type of attitude as "behaving like mere men" (1 Corinthians 3:3). Imagine becoming imitators of God in dispensing His grace to others instead of seeking for self. We need to become not only the recipients, but also the propagators of His glorious grace.

There are other times when we believe we deserve blessings from God because we perform what Richard Foster calls "spiritual disciplines." I certainly believe we should be diligent in "spiritual disciplines" such as praying, reading the Bible, etc. However, we must not get caught in the performance trap of these disciplines. Many think that because they perform some "spiritual discipline" that God is under obligation to do certain things for them. Conversely, they also think if they don't, then God won't come to the party either.

James Montgomery Boice illustrates this point when writing about R.A. Torrey, who was doing a series of meetings on prayer in Melbourne. He says that one day just before one of the meetings, Mr.Torrey was given a note that read:

Dear Mr. Torrey,

I am in great perplexity. I have been praying for a long time for something that I am confident is according to God's will, but do not get it. I have been a member of the Presbyterian Church for thirty years, and have tried to be a consistent one all the time. I have been superintendent in the Sunday school for twenty-five years, and an elder in the church for twenty years; and yet God does not answer my prayer and I cannot understand it. Can you explain it to me?

Boice recounts the great evangelist's reply, "This man thinks that because he has been a consistent church member for thirty years, a faithful Sunday school superintendent for twenty-five years, and an elder in the church for twenty years, that God is under obligation to answer his prayer. He is really praying in his own name, and God will not hear our prayers when we approach Him in that way. We must, if we would have God answer our prayers, give up any thought that we have any claims upon God. There is not one of us who deserves anything from God."[16]

When we pray or receive anything from God it is based purely on the merit of Christ. That is why we pray in His name and not our own. Paul, addressing the Romans on receiving from God, stated that God "who did not spare His own Son, but delivered Him up for us all, how shall He not with Him freely give us all things?" (Romans 8:32). We receive from God not through the discipline of prayer alone, but through the faith we have in the merit of Christ.

As a Christian you may ask the question like the Apostle Peter, "But don't I deserve something from God for all I've done?" Consider this: Do you really want God to reward you for what you deserve?

The Bible says, "the wages of sin is death, but the gift of God is eternal life in Christ Jesus our Lord" (Romans 6:23). David in the Psalms also says, "He has not dealt with us according to our sins, Nor punished us according to our iniquities" (Psalms 103:10).

Not only do Christians have this problem, but many people who are not yet Christians think, "If God was fair, then how could He send a good person like me or others to hell?" The problem is that they see themselves as good and not as they really are—separated from God because of their sin. God in a sense doesn't send anyone to hell; every individual was already separated from Him because of sin. It is only when we acknowledge that we have sinned against God that He can then show us how we can be rescued. It is not until we understand we are lost, that we discover we need to be found.

When we respond to God's invitation (like the workers in the parable), God doesn't give us what we deserve; He gives us what we need.

Imagine our lives if we would only see ourselves in this right perspective, with no claims or entitlements upon God. Then we would see the abundance of God's grace and we would continually live every moment out of a grateful heart. We couldn't help but thank God for everything and give thanks in every situation. What a different lifestyle we would lead. We would never need to complain about any circumstance, but would be forever grateful to a loving God who didn't give us what we truly deserved.

People Who See Themselves as Undeserving

Consider the workers that were hired for only part of the day. Some of these people would have seen themselves as undeserving compared to their effort.

The twelve-hour workers were hired at the rate of a denarius for the day. But each of the subsequent workers was hired on the agreement of being paid "what is right." These workers performed their duties for a fraction of the total day; some worked only one hour, others three, six and nine hours. When they were called up to receive their wages each of them received a denarius.

These workers would have noticed the twelve-hour workers receive a denarius as well. I'm sure the sweat-filled and soil-stained clothes of the twelve-hour workers caused many who hadn't performed as much work to feel guilty that they had received the same wage. Instead of being jubilant for what they had received, some would have been "eaten away" by a sense of guilt and unworthiness. The need to earn what they received surpassed the gratitude of the generosity given.

When we place ourselves in this position we subject ourselves to the following attitudes:

- We have an attitude that we must work to earn or deserve from God.

- We have an attitude of guilt and unworthiness instead of joy and gratitude.
- We place ourselves in a position of self-righteousness, thinking we can make it on our own. We don't need a "hand out."

What are the results of this type of thinking?
- The more we think we need to earn—the more we resist the hand of God.
- The more we think we don't deserve—the more guilty and condemned we become for what we do receive.

The Galatians had this type of attitude after so-called "Christian Jews" came down from Jerusalem. Paul chastised them for their works mentality by asking them, "This only I want to learn from you: Did you receive the Spirit by the works of the Law, or by the hearing of faith? Are you so foolish? Having begun in the Spirit, are you now being made perfect by the flesh? (Galatians 3:2–3). The Galatians were going back to a works mentality to secure their salvation.

Paul was instructing them that they didn't understand what they were doing. Going back under the Law to earn salvation by their works would bring them back into the bondage of sin and death. He says to them, "You have become estranged from Christ, you who attempt to be justified by the law; you have fallen from grace" (Galatians 5:4).

It is when we try to earn or work for any of God's gifts that we actually put ourselves outside of His grace. When instructing the Romans on this matter, Paul wrote, "And if by grace, then it is no longer of works; otherwise grace is no longer grace. But if it is of works, it is no longer grace; otherwise work is no longer work" (Romans 11:6). Everything that comes from God comes by His grace; therefore, we can no longer work for it.

Grace by its very definition means: the undeserved and unmerited favor of God. We don't deserve it and we can't earn it. The opposite of that statement reveals two prominent mentalities humanity tries to live by today.

Imagine a very generous and wealthy person coming up to you and giving you the keys to a brand new, top-of-the-line Mercedes Benz. Somewhat surprised by the stranger's generosity you are bewildered at the gift. Your mind automatically goes into thinking mode—"What have I done to deserve this?" Usually you can't think of anything you have done to deserve a gift from a stranger, so your mind then continues the thinking process, "What can I give them in return?" It is so difficult for us to think someone else will bless us simply out of the generosity of his or her heart. Our instinct tells us we need to give them something in return.

Try to picture the person's response as you reach into your pocket and pull out some money to give in return. Here he or she is giving you a very expensive gift and you hand over two dollars and forty-five cents. Can you see the horror and utter amazement on the person's face as you try to give something in return?

Our repayment plan in this story is as ludicrous as trying to do something for God in return for the gift of salvation. No matter how much work we could do, we would never come close to paying back the price it cost God to give Jesus for us. Yet, we continue with the mentality that we need to do works to earn blessings from God. We need to simply receive His wonderful gifts with a grateful heart and let them flow through us to touch other people and glorify Him.

People Who Gratefully Accept God's Grace

According to Mosaic law, the landowners were compelled to pay the workers that same day and not carry the wages over to another day (Leviticus 19:13, Deuteronomy 24:14–15). The primary reason was that these people were poor and needed to purchase food daily for their families.

Imagine now for a moment, you are a one-hour worker. The custom of the day stated that peasants with tools in hand, would gather before daybreak in the marketplace ready to start work at sunrise. The finishing time was at the appearing of the stars at night.[17]

You awaken while it is still the dark of night and get ready to make your way to the marketplace. After arriving at the meeting point, you see landowners from the region come and start hiring workers for the day. Knowing the need of your family, you try to look strong and enthusiastic. As workers are being chosen from all around you, your heart begins to grow discouraged. Every time you see a landowner approach, a fresh glimmer of hope arises, but to no avail. The day drags on and on; each minute seems like an eternity. With every minute that passes so does the opportunity to purchase the necessary essentials. Knowing there is no other avenue for you to earn wages, you continue to stick it out until the last possible moment.

Finally, with the sun going down on the horizon and only one-hour before the workday ends, you are hired and will be paid "what is right." The knowledge of receiving wages only for an hour hardly inspires you to do your best. You accompany the steward to the vineyard and join some of those with whom you had been standing throughout the day. You no sooner commence work than you see the first stars appear. To your surprise the steward calls you and the others that only worked for an hour up first to receive your wages.

You stretch forth your hand expecting to receive an "assarius" (a coin between a tenth and sixteenth of a denarius).[18] Instead, you are handed a denarius and you question the steward, "But I've only worked one hour, you must have given me the wrong coin." The steward reassures you that this is what the landowner desires to pay you. After the initial shock, imagine the gratitude and jubilation you feel toward this landowner. The discouragement during the day is turned into delight. The anxiousness of not being able to provide for your family is turned into appreciation. In one single act of kindness and generosity your life is turned around. We have the opportunity to turn every situation and circumstance into thanksgiving and joy when we are conscious of abiding in God's wonderful grace.

Unlike the first two types of people who responded to God's grace, the person who gratefully receives it without trying to deserve or earn it, places himself or herself in a position to receive more grace (James 4:6).

When we place ourselves in this position we subject ourselves to the following attitudes:

- We have an attitude that God's desire to give to us is based solely upon His grace.
- We have a continual attitude of gratitude and thankfulness.
- We place ourselves in a position of humility; not thinking higher or lower of ourselves.

What are the results of this type of thinking?

- The more we think we can't earn—the more we allow God to be God and His grace to flow.
- The more we think of what we truly deserve—the more thankful and grateful we become for what we have received.

Humility endears the grace of God and the grace of God endears a grateful heart. The one-hour workers not only received an abundance compared to what they deserved, but they also went away with an even greater measure of gratefulness and contentment. The twelve-hour workers may have received the agreed wage but they went away bankrupt in regard to gratitude.

Paul instructed Timothy to withdraw from "the proud. ...Who suppose that godliness is a means of gain," but he accentuates that "godliness with contentment is great gain" (1 Timothy 6:4–6).

The two responses that resist the grace of God are found in two scriptures:

- "God resists the *proud*, but gives *grace* to the humble" (James 4:6 emphasis added). Pride is the condition of those who put themselves in the position of the twelve hour workers.
- "For by *grace* are you have been saved through faith, and that not of yourselves; it is the gift of God, *not of works*,

lest anyone should boast" (Ephesians 2:8–9 emphasis added).

Pride is saying what I deserve. Works is saying what I need to do to earn and I don't need Your help.

It is only when we humble ourselves and see ourselves in the right perspective that we can see God in His proper perspective. God resists the proud, the ones who place themselves in their own self-righteousness (either deserving or needing to earn), but gives grace to the humble, those who see themselves as they really are. When we place ourselves in the position of the one-hour workers we see God in His true perspective:

- full of grace and mercy and
- full of love and compassion

Only then will we be forever grateful.

CHAPTER 12

GLORY

An old missionary couple had been working in Africa for years and was returning to New York City to retire. They had no pension; their health was broken; they were defeated, discouraged and afraid. They discovered they were booked on the same ship as President Teddy Roosevelt, who was returning from one of his big-game hunting expeditions.

No one paid any attention to the couple. They watched the fanfare that accompanied the President's entourage, as passengers tried to catch a glimpse of the great man.

As the ship moved across the ocean, the old missionary said to his wife, "Something is wrong. Why should we have given our lives in faithful service for God in Africa all these many years and have no one care a thing about us? Here this man comes back from a hunting trip and everybody makes such a fuss over him, but nobody gives two hoots about us."

"Dear, you shouldn't feel that way," his wife said.

"I can't help it; it doesn't seem right," he replied.

When the ship docked in New York, a band was waiting to greet the President. The mayor and other dignitaries were there. The papers were full of the President's arrival, but no one noticed the missionary couple. They slipped off the ship and found a cheap flat on the East Side, hoping the next day to see what they could do to make a living in the city.

That night the man's spirit broke. He said to his wife, "I can't take this; God is not treating us fairly."

His wife replied, "Why don't you go into the bedroom and tell that to the Lord?"

A short time later he came out from the bedroom, but now his face was completely different. His wife asked, "Dear, what happened?"

"The Lord settled it with me," he said. "I told him how bitter I was that the President should receive this tremendous homecoming, when no one met us as we returned home. And when I finished, it seemed as though the Lord put his hand on my shoulder and simply said, 'But you're not home yet!'"[19]

This story shows us the focus of what we are living for is three-fold: first, to bring glory to Jesus; second, understanding the glory of seeing others become all that God desires them to be; and, third, the glory we will receive for a job well done.

Jesus prays an incredible prayer in John 17. This is the prayer He prayed just before His prayer in the garden of Gethsemane:

Father, the hour has come. Glorify Your Son that Your Son also may glorify You ... I have glorified You on the earth. I have finished the work which You have given Me to do. And now, O Father, glorify Me together with Yourself, with the glory which I had with You before the world was (John 17:1, 4–5).

Jesus left the boundless glory that He possessed in heaven to come to this earth. While He was on earth, He brought glory to the Father through everything He did: through the way He lived, through the performing of miracles, through the words He taught, through the thoughts and feelings He had and through the way He treated others. Through all these things, Jesus brought glory to the Father.

Even though Jesus did everything for us, it was all to bring glory to the Father. When Jesus was about to finish His work, which He did in obedience to His Father, He said, "the hour has come. Glorify your Son." Jesus' time on earth was coming to a close. His time for glorifying the Father from earth was ending. Now it was Jesus' turn to be glorified again.

Jesus completed His work and just before He ascended into heaven, He told His disciples to wait in Jerusalem for the Holy Spirit. Jesus had been on the earth and given all glory to the Father. Now it was the Holy Spirit's turn to be in the earth. Jesus said of Him, "However when He, the Spirit of truth, has come, ... He will glorify Me" (John 16:13–14).

While on the earth, Jesus only did and said what He heard the Father tell Him to do. In that way, He glorified the Father. All He did was for the Father and by the Father. The Holy Spirit, in the same way, does nothing of Himself. Jesus said of Him, "He will take of what is Mine, and declare it to you" (John 16:16).

Once we are joined to the Lord, we are "one spirit with the Lord." Everything we do together with the Holy Spirit is to glorify Jesus. Jesus said of us, "I am glorified in them" (John 17:10).

When we preach the gospel, it is to testify and witness to the glory of Jesus. When we live bearing the fruit of the Spirit (love, joy, peace, etc.), it is to bring glory to Jesus. When we love one another as Jesus loved us, it is to bring glory to Jesus. When we overcome our trials, it is to bring glory to Jesus for making us overcomers. All we do, we do for the glory of Jesus, because "in Him we live and move and have our being" (Acts 17:28).

Glory and Honor Go Hand in Hand

But you do not have His word abiding in you, because whom He sent, Him you do not believe. You search the Scriptures, for in them you think you have eternal life; and these are they which testify of Me. But you are not willing to come to Me that you may have life. I do not receive honor from men. But I know you, that you do not have the love of God in you. I have come in My Father's name, and you do not receive Me; if another comes in his own name, him you will receive. How can you believe, who receive honor from one another, and do not seek the honor that comes from the only God? (John 5:38–44).

This passage of scripture declares to us that we cannot have the Word of God abiding in us if we do not believe in Jesus. On the other hand, the result of believing is the abiding of the Word of God within us. Together with this abiding comes true honor for God: if we abide in Him and His Word abides in us, we will bear much fruit. This is where the Father is truly glorified and honored (John 15:7–8).

How does fruit become evident through our lives? It becomes evident only when we are in Him and His Word is in us. Our whole focus must be upon Jesus and to bring all glory and honor to Him. Jesus upbraids the Jews by saying, "How can you believe, who receive honor from one another, and do not seek the honor that comes from the only God?" (John 5:44).

True belief, when resident within our lives, will not seek for man's approval. Our hearts will not exist to perform or impress. When we do something, it will be out of obedience to God and for His glory and honor.

The Christians at Corinth had the same battle as the Jews. Paul chastises them for "behaving like mere men" (1 Corinthians 3:3). They were seeking after the approval of man (in this instance, that of Paul or Apollos). He goes on to say, "Don't you know that all things are yours?" (1 Corinthians 3:21). The question he was putting forward to them was, "Why are you limiting yourselves to men and the approval of men when everything is yours?"

As Christians, we have been given everything that pertains to life and godliness. Once we are aware of this, Paul places emphasis not upon what we possess, but to whom we belong: "All [things] are yours. And you are Christ's and Christ is God's" (1 Corinthians 3:22–23). When we belong to God, all of His possessions are at our disposal—all His power, all His revelation, all His attributes and character, all His favor.

Paul then brings the Corinthians to a stark reality which we also need to heed: "For who makes you differ from another? And what do you have that you did not receive? Now if you did indeed receive it, why do you boast as if you had not received it?" (1 Corinthians 4:7).

The self-part of humanity is so prideful that it always wants to receive recognition. Thank God for the Holy Spirit who puts our fleshly nature to death. God's Spirit within us always brings us to the reality that God and only He shall receive all the glory. When we allow this to happen, the grace of God will continually be poured upon us. The humble are those who know who they are and what they possess, but not of themselves and not for themselves.

Let the reality of this scripture sink into your mind. Everything we have, we have received: our gifts, our abilities, the anointing within us, our calling and life purpose, our breath, the wisdom and knowledge we have, our eternal life, the Lord of Glory, Jesus Himself, the precious Holy Spirit and the day we have today. God has freely given us all things. How awesome and great is our God? Who could ever think to withhold any of the glory and honor He deserves? It all belongs to Him.

Withholding Honor Hinders God's Work

And when the Sabbath had come, He began to teach in the synagogue. And many hearing Him were astonished, saying, "Where did this Man get these things? And what wisdom is this which is given to Him, that such mighty works are performed by His hands! Is this not the carpenter, the Son of Mary, and brother of James, Joses, Judas, and Simon? And are not His sisters here with us?" So they were offended at Him.

But Jesus said to them, "A prophet is not without honor except in his own country, among his own relatives, and in his own house." Now he could do no mighty work there, except that He laid His hands on a few sick people and healed them. And He marveled because of their unbelief. Then He went about the villages in a circuit, teaching (Mark 6:2–6).

From this passage of scripture, we see that people are astounded at Jesus' teaching and at His miracles, but they refuse to believe anything about Him other than He is a carpenter and a member of a very common family. They would not honor Him for who He truly was: the Son of God, the Messiah.

This lack of belief and honor hindered Jesus so much that He could only heal a few sick people. When we do not honor God for who He is, we empower Him through our pride to resist us and withhold from us. But when we honor, esteem and believe Him, He pours out His grace and releases His abundance toward us.

God is longing to save, heal and deliver lives all across this world. If only humanity would empower Him through honor and belief. In Nazareth, He could only heal a few sick folks. How much more was He willing and desiring to do?

Imagine the blind people who could have received their sight, the deaf who could have heard their families for the first time, the crippled who could have walked the streets, the countless thousands who could have received eternal life. The Lord of Glory was right there among them and they stayed His hand. What miracles could have taken place? What are the possibilities that lay before us today or tomorrow? Who will our lives touch as we honor and give glory to God? Think of the things that God will enable you to do because you enabled and empowered Him through your honor of Him. You are His ambassador, His minister, His hands, His feet and His mouthpiece. You are His vessel unto honor.

The Glory We Desire for Others

In this section, we will again look at a number of passages Paul wrote. He was a selfless man who gave glory to God and sought glory for others; hence there was also laid up for him a crown of glory.

One of the most powerful prayers that Paul prayed is found in his letter to the Ephesians. He prayed, among other things, "that the eyes of your understanding being enlightened; that you may know what is the hope of His calling, [and] what are the riches of the glory of His inheritance in the saints" (Ephesians 1:18).

Many Christians read this passage of scripture in the light of eternity and what inheritance they will receive in Glory, but this passage is for the here and now. Paul prays that Christians would know the riches of the glory that are *in* us. When do the beneficiaries receive the inheritance from their loved one who has died? Certainly not when they themselves are dead, but while they are still alive.

Paul wants the saints to know the inheritance they now possess. This inheritance, which consists of the riches of the glory, is *in* them now.

What are the riches of the glory? The following verses list quite a number of riches. Let's count them.

Blessed be the God and Father of our Lord Jesus Christ, who has blessed us with every spiritual blessing in the heavenly places in Christ, just as He chose us in Him before the foundation of the world, that we should be holy and without blame before Him in love, having predestined us to adoption as sons by Jesus Christ to Himself, according to the good pleasure of His will, to the praise of the glory of His grace, by which He made us accepted in the Beloved. In Him we have redemption through His blood, the forgiveness of sins, according to the riches of His grace (Ephesians 1:3–7).

In these first seven verses we find six riches:

1. every spiritual blessing in heavenly places
2. holy and without blame before Him
3. adopted as sons and daughters of God
4. accepted in the Beloved
5. redemption through His blood
6. forgiveness of sins

That He would grant you, according to the riches of His glory, to be strengthened with might through His Spirit in the inner man, that Christ may dwell in your hearts through faith; that you, being rooted and grounded in love, may be able to comprehend with all the saints what is the width and length and depth and height—to know the love of Christ which passes knowledge; that you may be filled with all the fullness of God. Now to Him who is able to do exceedingly abundantly above all that we ask or think, according to the power that works in us, to Him be glory in the church by Christ Jesus to all generations, forever and ever. Amen (Ephesians 3:16–21).

Five more riches are found in these five verses:

7. strengthened with might in the inner man
8. rooted and grounded in love
9. ability to comprehend the love of God
10. filled with all the fullness of God
11. God able to do exceedingly abundantly above all we could ask or think according to the power that is at work in us

And my God shall supply all your need according to His riches in glory by Christ Jesus (Philippians 4:19).

The twelfth one is:

12. supply all your needs according to heaven's glories, not earth's.

To them God willed to make known what are the riches of the glory of this mystery among the Gentiles: which is Christ in you, the hope of glory (Colossians 1:27).

The last two are:
13. know the riches of glory
14. Christ in you, the hope of glory

Paul's desire, by revealing the riches of glory, is that he "may present every man perfect in Christ Jesus." These words, together with those he spoke to the Thessalonians, sum up his life and ministry for others: "For what is our hope, or joy, or crown of rejoicing? Is it not even you in the presence of our Lord Jesus Christ at His coming? For you are our glory and joy" (1 Thessalonians 2:19–20).

He did not "seek glory from men" (1 Thessalonians 2:6), but that people would walk worthy of God, who calls them "into His own kingdom and glory" (1 Thessalonians 2:12). He had such a heart for people that he said, "I could wish that I myself were accursed from Christ for my brethren, my country men according to the flesh, who are Israelites to whom pertain the adoption, the glory" (Romans 9:3–4).

Paul is an outstanding example to each of us. He sought to bring glory to God by seeing others inherit the riches of the glory. No matter what came Paul's way, his focus was for others to turn toward God. He said to Timothy in some of his final words, "I endure all things for the sake of the elect, that they also may obtain salvation which is in Christ Jesus with eternal glory" (2 Timothy 2:10).

Can you sense the heart of Paul for others? The epitome of selfishness would be to embrace all that God has for us in salvation and to enter the courts of heaven alone: "For unless a grain of wheat falls to the ground and dies it abides alone." Always seek to strive and endure for others, that they may receive the riches of glory before us. Let us, together with Paul, have a passion so embedded within us that we would seek glory for others as a higher priority than glory for ourselves. God is truly glorified in lives that have attitudes and hearts such as this.

The Glory We Shall Receive

A crown of glory awaits those who glorify God and strive to promote others to glory. Our cause is always to bring glory to God and others to glory; the effect is a "crown of glory." Our goal is to honor God by treasuring people; our prize is the "glory we shall receive."

My intention in this final section is not to focus solely on the "glory we shall receive," but to point us to the fact that what we have and what we shall receive is not of ourselves; it is all of God. Even when we receive our rewards we will, together with the twenty-four elders, cast our crowns before the throne saying:

You are worthy, O Lord, to receive glory and honor and power; For You created all things, and by Your will they exist and were created (Revelation 4:11).

We have shared much concerning the foundation of our Christianity throughout this book. We have learned there is no foundation that can be laid other than Jesus, Himself. Once the foundation is laid, we can commence building upon it. God warns us, though, through Paul, to take heed how we build, because each one's works will be tested: "If anyone's work which he has built on it endures, he will receive a reward" (1 Corinthians 3:14).

We have only one opportunity in life to build for Jesus and His kingdom. The result of what we do during our time on earth will forever seal our eternal future in the kingdom of heaven. Think deeply about this statement. What you have done and what you will continue to do are all working toward one special day, a day when you will be changed to an immortal being. From that moment, there will be no further opportunity to add an extra grade to your results. You will have graduated forever to glory with the rewards you have earned.

That will be a very special day, which will result in the substance of your glorified, resurrected body. Paul describes it this way: "There is one glory of the sun, another glory of the moon, another glory of the stars; for one star differs from another star in glory. So also is the resurrection of the dead" (1 Corinthians 15:41–42). Each one will receive a glorified body with different variations of glory depending on how we have lived here on earth. Some will glow brighter than others in intensity of glory.

No wonder Paul encouraged the saints to endure trials and work righteousness. He said:

> Therefore we do not lose heart. Even though our outward man is perishing, yet the inward man is being renewed day by day. For our light affliction, which is but for a moment, is working for us *a far more exceeding and eternal weight of glory*, while we do not look at the things which are seen, but at the things which are not seen. For the things which are seen are temporary, but the things which are not seen are eternal (2 Corinthians 4:16–18 emphasis added).

Jesus also encouraged the disciples in a similar manner. He said, "Do not lay up for yourselves treasures on earth, where moth and rust destroy and where thieves break in and steal; but lay up for yourselves treasures in heaven, where neither moth nor rust destroys and where thieves do not break in and steal" (Matthew 6:19–20).

The great faith chapter of the Bible also makes reference to this amazing subject. "Women received their dead to life again. Others were tortured, not accepting deliverance, that they might obtain a better resurrection" (Hebrews 11:35).

You have only one opportunity to live your life. Make sure your foundation is secure in Jesus. When your foundation is secure, you will have little concern for yourself. You will be free to focus on the call of God for your life.

Don't get caught up trying to save your own life. Know that Jesus has authored your faith. Know that you will be kept by His power through faith. Know that He has provided you with all the resources and the time to do all that He has purposed for you to do. Know that you can do it. Know that you will do it—and do it with the abundance of grace He has poured out over your life.

END NOTES

1. Chinoy, Mike, (2000), *CNN Report—Taiwan Still Struggling to Rebuild from 1999 Quake*, www.cnn.com/2000/asianow/east/09/20/taiwan.quake.
2. Spurgeon, Charles Haddon, *All of Grace* (New Kensington: Whitaker House, 1981), p.104.
3. Strong, James, *The Exhaustive Concordance of the Bible*, Strong's Number: 3340.
4. Hunt, Gladys, *Does Anyone Here Know God?* (Grand Rapids: Zondervan Publishing House 1967), p. 45. Used by permission.
5. Seamands, David A., *Healing Grace: Finding Freedom from the Performance Trap* (Indianapolis: Light & Life Communications, 1999), p. 200–201. Used by permission.
6. Kik, Jacob Marcellus, *Sermon on the Cup of Gethsemane*, www.abcog.org/cup.htm.
7. Tan, Paul Lee, *Encyclopedia of 7700 Illustrations* (Rockville, Maryland: Assurance Publishers, 1979) p. 1091.
8. Brengle, Samuel Logan. *Heart Talks on Holiness* (Atlanta: The Salvation Army Supplies and Purchasing Department, 1897) p. 57.
9. Baxter, Richard, *The Free Gift* www.sermonillustrations.com/a-z/g/grace_gods.htm
10. Bromiley, Geoffry W., General Editor. *International Standard Bible Encyclopaedia Vol. 4.* (Grand Rapids: William B. Eerdmans, 1988), p. 136.
11. Author unknown.
12. Finney, Charles G., edited by William Ernest Allen, *Sanctification and Fifty-four Relations of Christ to Christians* (Fort Washington: Christian Literature Crusade), p. 13. Used by permission.
13. Powell, John, et al., *Unconditional Love* (Allen, Texas: Argus Communication, 1995), p. 50.

14. Bridges, Jerry, *Transforming Grace* (Colorado Springs, Navpress, 1993), p. 67–68. Used by permission of NavPress (www.navpress.com). All rights reserved.
15. Ibid., 69.
16. Boice, James Montgomery, *The Parables of Jesus* (Chicago: Moody Press, 1983), p. 62–63. As quoted in R.A. Torrey, *The Power of Prayer and the Prayer of Power* (Grand Rapids: Zondervan, 1955), p. 138–139.
17. Freeman, James M., *The New Manners & Customs of the Bible* (North Brunswick: Bridge-Logos Publishers, 1998), p. 449. Used by permission.
18. Ibid., 448.
19. Stedman, Ray C., *Talking to My Father* (Grand Rapids: Discovery House Publishers, 1997), p.27–28. Used by permission.

STUDY GUIDE

Each lesson in this study guide relates to the respective chapters throughout the book. They have been specifically designed to help you grow and develop in these foundational principles of Christianity. As with anything we do in life, we get out of it what we put into it. You have already invested in purchasing this book to help you grow and develop. Get all that you can out of it.

My desire is to see you grow and develop in every aspect represented in this material. I don't want to fill you with knowledge only, but as Jesus told His disciples, "Go therefore and make disciples ... *teaching them to observe* all things that I have commanded you" (Matthew 28:19a–20a). I desire that you not only know what Jesus wants you to learn, but also that you observe and put it into practice.

Sometimes we gain knowledge about a certain point or subject, but move on to another aspect before we've had a chance to put the last one into practice. Jesus told us to teach each other to observe what He said, not just teach what He said. By learning something and then moving on to the next thing, before putting the first one into practice, we are declaring that knowledge is more important than obedience. What Jesus desires of us, however, is not that we acquire knowledge, but that we gain a new life and a new lifestyle through obedience.

The study guide can be used effectively either in a group situation or personally. Group leaders should encourage all members to build the principles of one lesson into their lives before proceeding to the next. It's better to spend a couple weeks effectively developing one topic in each life, than to know the material without producing lasting fruit.

The study guides contain four key sections. The following information explains how to make the best use of the material.

Personal Application

Jesus doesn't expect us to become perfect overnight; He spent three years establishing the foundation of the lives of the apostles. The apostles then spent the rest of their lives growing from that foundation. There are many aspects of the Christian life in which we need to grow and develop. The main thing is to establish and put into practice one or two areas at a time.

> But be doers of the word, and not hearers only, deceiving yourselves ... But he who looks into the perfect law of liberty and continues in it, and is not a forgetful hearer but a doer of the work, this one will be blessed in what he does (James 1:22, 25).

> They profess to know God, but in works they deny Him, being abominable, disobedient, and disqualified for every good work. But as for you, speak the things which are proper for sound doctrine ... in all things showing yourself to be a pattern of good works; in doctrine showing integrity, reverence, incorruptibility, sound speech that cannot be condemned, that one who is an opponent may be ashamed, having nothing evil to say of you (Titus 1:16, 2:1, 7–8).

It is better to develop one or two aspects of Christ-like nature at a time and achieve growth in those areas, than to work on many aspects and never see any fruit at all. Each week try to develop one particular aspect of Christianity from either the areas suggested, or those you feel you need to develop.

Principle Truths to Dwell On

For each chapter I have identified key principles to activate your memory. They formulate a good checklist to assist you in incorporating major principles into life-forming habits, as you are studying the guide. They can also be used as a checkup at regular intervals throughout your life. Each of these truths is timeless and fundamental to our development. Come back and review them often.

If you are unsure of the answer to a particular question, read through the chapter again until you find the relevant section.

Renewing Your Inner Being

During the course of each study you will be prompted with the following suggestion: Outline two areas you've identified in this study to build into your life over the next few weeks. Remember, don't believe you have learned something simply by identifying it or hearing about it. The test of learning is being able to "do." What we learn must become second nature to us.

This exercise is placed in each chapter's study guide to deliberately keep you growing and developing. Don't grow familiar with it and just pass over it. It is far too important to miss. Our actions come from who we are on the inside, and applying this principle to our lives develops us from the inside.

You may like to re-read chapter eight to identify these key concepts again.

Key Scriptures for Memory and Meditation

Joshua 1:8 says, "This Book of the Law shall not depart from your mouth, but you shall meditate in it day and night, that you may observe to do according to all that is written in it. For then you will make your way prosperous, and then you will have good success."

Again Psalm 1:1–3 says, "Blessed is the man Who walks not in the counsel of the ungodly, Nor stands in the path of sinners, Nor sits in the seat of the scornful; But his delight is in the law of the Lord, And in His law he meditates day and night. He shall be like a tree Planted by the rivers of water, That brings forth fruit in its season, Whose leaf shall not wither; And whatsoever he does shall prosper."

Committing the Word of God to memory will build your life in the following ways: First, "faith comes by hearing and hearing by the word of God" (Romans 10:17). Every time you hear the Word of God your faith develops. Second, everything other than the Word of God will pass away, so what you build into your life from the Scriptures will last forever. Third, when temptations or trials come your way, you can answer them immediately with the Word of God. Jesus did this when tempted by the devil in Matthew 4. Fourth, the Bible says, "Man shall not live by bread alone, but by every word that proceeds from the mouth of God." The Word of God is what we live by for sustenance. If you commit the Word of God to memory you will be prompted to live the right way all day, every day. Fifth, when sharing Jesus with those in need, you may not have access to a Bible. Committing verses to memory will allow you to share with others as the need arises, not just your opinions, but also the Word of God.

Bible Study

Forming the habit of reading and studying the Word of God is one of the most profitable things you can do. Paul said to Timothy in Second Timothy 2:15, "Be diligent to present yourself approved to God, a worker who does not need to be ashamed, rightly dividing the word of truth." The Bible is God's manual on how to live. We need to know, understand and do what the manual says in order to live the right way.

One method for studying passages of scripture is to read a whole chapter (to gain an overall understanding within a certain context) and then go back to the begining and read through the text verse-by-verse again. As you go through the text the second time, have a pad and pen handy and ask yourself questions concerning each verse:

- What can I know about God in this verse?
- What is God saying to me in this verse?
- How could I apply this thought to my life?
- Is there anything about this verse that I don't understand that I need to ask someone?

Prayer

Studying the Word of God is important, so that we know God, we understand God and are transformed into His nature. Equally important is praying. Praying is talking to God. There is no special way to pray; just be yourself and talk honestly to God from your heart.

We pray to God our Father in the same way a son or daughter would talk to his or her father (in a model family). When we are born again into God's family, He becomes our dad. A father provides for his children, teaches them, encourages them, sets the example for them and corrects and disciplines them. A child on the other hand, honors, respects, listens, obeys, imitates and gives his or her father thanks, just to mention a few proper responses. Relationships like these only develop because the children are continually talking to and spending time with their father. This is what prayer is all about—developing a relationship with our Heavenly Father, getting to know Him and honoring Him through obedience.

When talking to God, whom we cannot see, we can easily lose our focus because of distractions we see around us. You may find writing out your key thoughts will help you stay focused on God and what you desire to pray for each day.

While working through this study, continue to develop your relationship with God through prayer and reading your Bible.

Chapter One
Jesus, Our Firm Foundation

Personal Application

Describe how you came to believe in Jesus.

List, if you can, any parts of you that were, or still are, in the foundation with Jesus.

In what way do you believe those parts of you can be taken out of the foundation if they aren't already?

What was your understanding of repentance when you first came to faith in Christ? Did that hinder you? How would you handle that now?

Describe the true nature of repentance and its place in the authoring of someone's faith.

What are the fundamental aspects of how a person is born again?

How would you now share Jesus with unsaved people to see them come to faith in Him?

Principle Truths

- If your salvation rests on Jesus alone, then you can be totally assured that the foundation of your salvation is secure.

- If there is any part of us in the foundation, we'll always feel insecure and have reason to doubt.

- The only common denominator for salvation after repentance (a change of thinking or a turning toward God) is, "Believe on the Lord Jesus."

- It is not our confession of faith that saves us, but our possession of faith in Jesus.

Renewing Your Inner Being

Outline two work areas you've identified in this study to build into your life over the next few weeks. Remember, don't believe you have learned something simply by identifying it or hearing about it. The test of learning is being able to "do." What we learn must become second nature to us.

Key Scriptures for Memory and Meditation

- "Believe on the Lord Jesus Christ and you will be saved" (Acts 16:31).

- "For by grace you have been saved though faith, and that not of yourselves: it is the gift of God, not of works, lest anyone should boast" (Ephesians 2:8–9).

CHAPTER TWO
LEARNING RIGHTEOUSNESS

Personal Application

Can you describe two fundamental aspects of what happened on the Cross? Two things were revealed and one can't be revealed to us without the other. What are those two aspects and how would you describe them and their influence on our lives?

How are we to learn the righteousness of God?

The Bible says that when we show grace to a wicked person they will not learn righteousness. What is the proper way to lead these people into the righteousness of God?

Jesus made a very powerful statement to Simon the Pharisee: "To whom little is forgiven the same will love little." What does that statement mean to you now having read this chapter? How can such a statement help you to love and serve God more?

Principle Truths

- Acknowledging your sin against God and the punishment it deserves, places you in an attitude of humility before God whose desire is to show you mercy.

- When you believe that Jesus took your place in receiving the total punishment of God for your sin, it frees you from all guilt and condemnation. Until that punishment has been totally finalized, there will never be a freedom to walk in His love and righteousness.

- When you understand the love and forgiveness of God, you are free to love and live for Him in the same proportion.

Renewing Your Inner Being

Outline two work areas you have identified in this study to build into your life over the next few weeks. Remember, don't believe you have learned something simply by identifying it or hearing about it. The test of learning is being able to "do." What we learn must become second nature to us.

Key Scriptures for Memory and Meditation

- "For I am not ashamed of the gospel of Christ, for it is the power of God to salvation for everyone who believes, for the Jew first and also for the Greek. For in it the righteousness of God is revealed from faith to faith; as it is written, 'The just shall live by faith.' For the wrath of God is revealed from heaven against all ungodliness and unrighteousness of men, who suppress the truth in unrighteousness" (Romans 1:16–18).

- "For when Your judgments are in the earth, the inhabitants of the world will learn righteousness" (Isaiah 26:9b).

- "Let grace be shown to the wicked, yet he will not learn righteousness; in the land of uprightness he will deal unjustly and will not behold the majesty of the Lord" (Isaiah 26:10).

- "But to whom little is forgiven, the same loves little" (Luke 7: 47b).

CHAPTER THREE
BELIEVING UNTO SALVATION

Personal Application

What has been your perspective about being "born again?" Being born again gives us security but not a false security. Describe the difference.

There are many scriptures that talk about believing and salvation. Can you identify some of them and explain the similarities and the differences of the two terms?

God gives clear examples of what happened to the children of Israel to warn us of certain things concerning believing and salvation. What is God trying to instruct us in concerning faith and believing?

Many people start the Christian walk but do not finish. After studying this chapter, how could you share your faith more effectively to enhance the possibility of someone finishing the race?

What is the primary thing you have to do to inherit the salvation that will be revealed in the end time?

When considering the life of the Apostle Paul, what was his primary focus for those who came to faith in Jesus? How can his example impact your life and your focus for other Christians?

Principle Truths

- Initially saying that Jesus is Lord doesn't automatically secure our salvation.

- Jesus is to be both the author and the finisher of our faith.

- Salvation is a result of receiving the end of your faith.

162

Renewing Your Inner Being

Outline two work areas you've identified in this study to build into your life over the next few weeks. Remember, don't believe you have learned something simply by identifying it or hearing about it. The test of learning is being able to "do." What we learn must become second nature to us.

Key Scriptures for Memory and Meditation

- "Looking unto Jesus the author and finisher of our faith" (Hebrews 12:2).

- "Receiving the end of your faith—the salvation of your souls" (1 Peter 1:9).

CHAPTER FOUR
OUR IDENTITY

Personal Application

How many times have you questioned whether you were still in relationship with God after you had done something drastically wrong? Some Christians never doubt their relationship with God but by far the majority do. Does your identity come from who you are or what you do? How can you change it if it is wrong?

In such a performance-orientated world, much of our acceptance comes from how well we do. What do you now understand in relation to performance and acceptance from God's perspective?

What is one of the biggest temptations we need to resist as a Christian? How do we go about this?

Humanity is supposed to be like God, yet how is this so? God says, "Be holy, for I am holy." How is this to become a reality? Discuss "trying to be" compared to "being."

Many things try to shape our identity. What is the one true way according to God's word?

What are the three ways the devil attempts to destroy God's word from taking root and producing fruit within our lives? Describe some of the different situations where this has actually happened to you and how you can identify the devil's attempts in the future.

Principle Truths

- The proof of our identity is in our birth record, not our performance.

- God's approval of us doesn't rest upon what we do, but upon who we are.

- The devil tempts us to prove that we are a son or daughter of God by what we do.

- Satan comes to steal God's word out of our heart.

- Persecution arises for the Word's sake. Do we really believe?

- Worldly things can cause us to be unfruitful.

- Take heed what we hear for with the same measure that we hear it, it will be measured to us again.

Renewing Your Inner Being

Outline two work areas you've identified in this study that you could build into your life over the next few weeks. Remember, don't believe you've learned something simply by identifying it or hearing about it. The test of learning is being able to "do." What we learn must become second nature to us.

Key Scriptures for Memory and Meditation

- "He has made us accepted in the Beloved" (Ephesians 1:6b).

- "This is My beloved Son in whom I am well pleased" (Matthew 3:17).

- "For as he [a man] thinks in his heart, so is he" (Proverbs 23:7).

- "Take heed what you hear. With the same measure you use, it will be measured to you; and to you who hear, more will be given" (Mark 4:24).

CHAPTER FIVE
RIGHTLY DIVIDING THE WORD OF TRUTH

Personal Application

Describe ways you have been confused when hearing or reading the Word of God.

What is your understanding of the Old Covenant compared to the New Covenant? Why did God have two Covenants? Bear in mind the first showed us sin; the second redeemed us from sin.

What did each of the Covenants produce?

Identify and memorize five key facts of the Old Covenant law.

Outline the roles of law and grace, clarifying whether they negate each other.

Describe the difference between a slave and a son in relation to this chapter.

In summary, is the ultimate goal of grace any different in result and action from the purpose of the Law? Please explain.

Principle Truths

- We need to rightly divide the Word of truth into the Old Covenant and New Covenant.
- We need to compare spiritual things with spiritual and natural things with natural.

Renewing Your Inner Being

Outline two work areas you've identified in this study to build into your life over the next few weeks. Remember, don't believe you have learned something simply by identifying it or hearing about it. The test of learning is being able to "do." What we learn must become second nature to us.

Key Scriptures for Memory and Meditation

- "Be diligent to present yourself approved to God, a worker who does not need to be ashamed, rightly dividing the word of truth" (2 Timothy 2:15).

- "These things we also speak, not in the words which man's wisdom teaches but which the Holy Spirit teaches, comparing spiritual things with spiritual. But the natural man does not receive the things of the Spirit of God, for they are foolishness to him; nor can he know them, because they are spiritually discerned" (1 Corinthians 2:13–14).

- "For the law was given through Moses, but grace and truth came through Jesus Christ" (John 1:17).

- "For sin shall not have dominion over you, for you are not under law but under grace" (Romans 6:14).

- "For you, brethren, have been called to liberty; only do not use liberty as an opportunity for the flesh, but through love serve one another" (Galatians 5:13).

CHAPTER SIX

WALKING IN THE SPIRIT

Personal Application

Before reading this chapter, how did you define living in the flesh or sinful nature? Knowing now that the flesh nature feeds and survives by feeding off of the "Tree of the Knowledge of Good and Evil," what would you add to your definition of living in the flesh?

What are some of the ramifications of living under the Law?

What are the goals of your flesh and spirit natures and how do they contend with each other?

Suppose I make the statement, "Jesus disarmed the demonic principalities and powers of their right to judge us or condemn us according to the Law." What does this mean for you now?

How does feeding off the "Tree of Life" enable you to do good works and put to death the deeds of the flesh?

Principle Truths

- Our old fleshly nature has been crucified with Christ.
- The Law, which kept our sinful nature alive, has also been put to death on the Cross.
- The flesh wants to be right with God and inherit what our spirit has—righteousness—though the flesh wants to attain it by itself.
- Jesus disarmed the demonic principalities and powers of their right to judge us or condemn us according to the Law.
- God's grace never abolishes the necessity of good works, rather, it enables them.

Renewing Your Inner Being

Outline two work areas you've identified in this study to build into your life over the next few weeks. Remember, don't believe you have learned something simply by identifying it or hearing about it. The test of learning is being able to "do." What we learn must become second nature to us.

Key Scriptures for Memory and Meditation

- "Walk in the Spirit and you shall not fulfill the lust of the flesh" (Galatians 5:16).

- "Are you so foolish? Having begun in the Spirit, are you now being made perfect by the flesh?" (Galatians 3:3).

- "You have become estranged from Christ, you who attempt to be justified by the law; you have fallen from grace" (Galatians 5:4).

CHAPTER SEVEN
THE HOLY SPIRIT'S PURPOSE
IN OUR LIVES

Personal Application

According to John 16:9, whom does the Holy Spirit convict of sin? What does this now say to you? Why do you feel you are convicted at times? Read Jeremiah 31:33–34.

Of what two things does the Holy Spirit desire to convict believers?

How will you allow the Holy Spirit to do His proper work in your life considering you have previously felt His purpose was to do the opposite?

What do you think will be the result of being firmly convinced you are righteous because Jesus has ascended to heaven on your behalf? How will that benefit you?

When you're fully convinced of your authority because the prince of this world has been judged, what do you believe you can do in God?

Principle Truths

- The Holy Spirit convicts unbelievers of sin to bring them to Jesus.
- The Holy Spirit convicts us of righteousness because Jesus has gone to the Father with His Blood to cover our sins.
- The Holy Spirit convicts us of judgment because the prince of this world (the devil) has been judged and God's judgment has given us back our authority over the earth.

Renewing Your Inner Being

Outline two work areas you've identified in this study to build into your life over the next few weeks. Remember, don't believe you have learned something simply by identifying it or hearing about it. The test of learning is being able to "do." What we learn must become second nature to us.

Key Scriptures for Memory and Meditation

- "And when He has come, He will convict the world of sin, and of righteousness, and of judgment: of sin, because they do not believe in Me; of righteousness, because I go to My Father and you see Me no more; of judgment, because the ruler of this world is judged" (John 16:8–11).

- "[Jesus] who Himself bore our sins in His own body on the tree, [did so] that we, having died to sins, might live for righteousness" (1 Peter 2:24a).

- "For you were once darkness, but now you are light in the Lord" (Ephesians 5:8a).

- "All authority has been given to Me in heaven and on earth. Go therefore … " (Matthew 28:18–19a).

CHAPTER EIGHT
REPENTANCE, RENEWAL AND RESTITUTION

Personal Application

Why can't trying to change your behavior alone work to produce lasting change within your life?

Describe the process of how a stronghold is formed in our life.

Outline how you would go about replacing a wrong stronghold with a right stronghold.

What is the end result of this process and how is a lasting change made to our behavior?

Are you continually reminded of any sins that you have committed in the past? It is very likely that even though you have confessed it to God, you may need to confess it to someone else so that you may be healed or you may need to make some kind of restitution. Pray and ask God what you should do in these cases. Remember, strive to live with a clear conscience before both God and men.

Principle Truths

- Repentance is all about a change of mind or a change of thinking, which results in a change of behavior.

- Strongholds both good and bad reside in our heart.

- We replace strongholds by taking thoughts captive to Christ and renewing our mind.

- Continue to stand firm in God until the new stronghold is formed and the other destroyed. This creates lasting change.

- Always live with a conscience having no offense toward God and men.

Renewing Your Inner Being

Outline two work areas you've identified in this study to build into your life over the next few weeks. Remember, don't believe you have learned something simply by identifying it or hearing about it. The test of learning is being able to "do." What we learn must become second nature to us.

Key Scriptures for Memory and Meditation

- "Put off, concerning your former conduct, the old man which grows corrupt according to the deceitful lusts, and be renewed in the spirit of your mind, and that you put on the new man which was created according to God, in true righteousness and true holiness" (Ephesians 4:22–24).

- "For though we walk in the flesh, we do not war according to the flesh. For the weapons of our warfare are not carnal but mighty in God for pulling down strongholds, casting down arguments and every high thing that exalts itself against the knowledge of God, bringing every thought into captivity to the obedience of Christ, and being ready to punish all disobedience when your obedience is fulfilled" (2 Corinthians 10:3–6).

- "Therefore take up the whole armor of God, that you may be able to withstand in the evil day, and having done all, to stand" (Ephesians 6:13).

- "This being so, I myself always strive to have a conscience without offense toward God and men" (Acts 24:16).

Chapter Nine
Kept by the Power of God

Personal Application

This world's tendency is to ensnare our lives. Who are the three persons who play a role in your life being kept? What are their roles?

Predominantly we have thought we have been the masters over our own lives. What are the two things that are stronger than mankind? How do they govern us?

What has been your process of overcoming sin? Charles Finney says Christians put efforts in this direction and that direction, and patch up their righteousness on the one side, while they make a rent in the other side. How has this been similar to your experience? What is the correct process in dealing with sin?

After reading this chapter, what does it now mean for you to be "in Christ?"

Why did God destroy the people of Israel? In what ways does this example instruct us?

What is the Holy Spirit's role in keeping you?

Principle Truths

- We cannot keep ourselves alone. We are primarily kept by the power of God and that takes place when we put our faith in Him to do so.

- The number one thing that disqualifies Christian lives is their faith or more importantly their lack of it.

- Have faith in God and doubt the devil's ability.

- The righteous requirements of the Law are fulfilled *in us* as we walk according to the Holy Spirit.

- We don't possess spiritual power we can utilize on our own; rather, the Holy Spirit is always releasing it through us but never independent from Himself.

- When we are in Christ, we are in faith and are being protected by Him.

Renewing Your Inner Being

Outline two work areas you've identified in this study to build into your life over the next few weeks. Remember, don't believe you have learned something simply by identifying it or hearing about it. The test of learning is being able to "do." What we learn must become second nature to us.

Key Scriptures for Memory and Meditation

- "Who are kept by the power of God through faith for salvation ready to be revealed in the last time" (1 Peter 1:5).

- "Examine yourselves as to whether you are in the faith. Prove yourselves. Do you not know yourselves, that Jesus Christ is in you?—unless indeed you are disqualified" (2 Corinthians 13:5).

- "I have fought the good fight, I have finished the race, I have kept the faith. Finally, there is laid up for me the crown of righteousness" (2 Timothy 4:7–8).

- "Now to Him who is able to keep you from stumbling, and to present you faultless before the presence of His glory with exceeding joy" (Jude 24).

- "But the Lord is faithful, who will establish you and guard you from the evil one" (2 Thessalonians 3:3).

CHAPTER TEN
FAITH THAT WORKS BY LOVE

Personal Application

How much of the love in your heart has been directed towards yourself?

In what areas of your life have you "drawn the line in the sand?" What things will now exist because of your unconditional love and what things can never exist anymore in regard to your relationship with God and others?

How successful are you? How successful do you want to be? Love never fails. How can you allow love to operate through your life more?

How often do you do things because of consequences toward yourself, whether good or bad? How can you change your focus to do things by focusing on what will benefit others?

Principle Truths

- Take the focus off yourself. Love others.
- Love seeks not its own.
- Unconditional love produces a birth and a death—something is and something will never be.
- Faith believes because love believes all things.
- When we do things out of rules and regulations, we do it for ourselves to avoid the consequences. When we do something out of love, we do it for the other person.

Renewing Your Inner Being

Outline two work areas you've identified in this study to build into your life over the next few weeks. Remember, don't believe you have learned something simply by identifying it or hearing about it. The test of learning is being able to "do." What we learn must become second nature to us.

Key Scriptures for Memory and Meditation

- "Faith working through love" (Galatians 5:6)
- "[Love] bears all things, believes all things, hopes all things, endures all things. Love never fails" (1 Corinthians 13:7–8).

CHAPTER ELEVEN
LIVING UNDER GOD'S GRACE

Personal Application

How often (like the twelve-hour workers in the parable) have you thought God was unfair to you? In what ways have you seen Him like that and can you now see Him from a better perspective?

Dwell upon what you truly deserve from God and then dwell upon the abundance of His grace. Make sure you see the clear contrast. The more you can see both of these opposite poles, the more you will see God as He truly is. Read Philippians 3:8–10 and begin to see what Paul saw.

How has the example of evangelist, R.A. Torrey, shown you that it's not your merit, but Jesus' merit that God is looking to reward?

You may have been like some of the other workers who considered themselves not worthy to receive from God without doing something for Him. Have you ever felt like this in the past and can you now see that your efforts alone were like filthy rags?

When we place ourselves in the position of the one-hour workers we see God in His true perspective, full of grace and mercy and full of love and compassion. Describe what life would be like for you if you always responded to it from the perspective of God's grace.

Principle Truths

- The more we think we have earned—the more we think God is unjust and resist His hand.

- The more we think we deserve—the more ungrateful we become for what we do receive and the more guilty and condemned we become for what we receive.

- The more we think we can't earn—the more we allow God to be God and His grace to flow.

- The more we think of what we truly deserve—the more thankful and grateful we become for what we have received.

Renewing Your Inner Being

Outline two work areas you've identified in this study to build into your life over the next few weeks. Remember, don't believe you have learned something simply by identifying it or hearing about it. The test of learning is being able to "do." What we learn must become second nature to us.

Key Scriptures for Memory and Meditation

- "God resists the proud, but gives grace to the humble" (James 4:6).

- "For by grace you have been saved through faith, and that not of yourselves; it is the gift of God, not of works, lest anyone should boast" (Ephesians 2:8–9).

CHAPTER TWELVE
GLORY

Personal Application

How would you describe glory and what do you believe the Bible means by glorifying Jesus in all we do?

How does seeking glory for ourselves work for the detriment of everything?

What do we enable by giving glory and honor to God?

What does seeking to promote others to glory do in us?

We have only one opportunity in life to build for Jesus and His kingdom. The result of what we do during our time on earth will forever seal our eternal future in the kingdom of heaven. Think deeply about this statement. What you have done and what you will continue to do are all working toward one special day, a day when you will be changed to an immortal being sealed with an eternal weight of glory. From that moment, there will be no further opportunity to add an extra grade to your results. You will have graduated forever to glory with the rewards you have earned. Discuss how thinking upon these lines will change your outlook on life.

Now that God has done all for you, free yourself to do all for Him and others. How do you plan to do this practically?

Principle Truths

- All we do, we do for the glory of Jesus.
- Withholding glory and honor from God hinders His work.
- Seek to bring glory to God by seeing others inherit the riches of glory.
- A crown of glory awaits those who glorify God and strive to promote others to glory.

Renewing Your Inner Being

Outline two work areas you've identified in this study to build into your life over the next few weeks. Remember, don't believe you have learned something simply by identifying it or hearing about it. The test of learning is being able to "do." What we learn must become second nature to us.

Key Scriptures for Memory and Meditation

- "I endure all things for the sake of the elect, that they also may obtain the salvation which is in Christ Jesus with eternal glory" (2 Timothy 2:10).

- "For our light affliction, which is but for a moment, is working for us a far more exceeding and eternal weight of glory" (2 Corinthians 4:17).

ABOUT THE AUTHOR

Brian Mulheran and his wife Vivienne, live in Brisbane, Australia, with their three children Benjamin, Kate, and Matthew. He is a Senior Executive Pastor at Citipointe Christian Outreach Centre and has been on staff there for fifteen years. The church is one of Australia's largest and fastest growing churches. Brian is also the Principal and a lecturer of Citipointe International Institute of Ministry, the premier Bible College of the Christian Outreach Centre Movement.

Citipointe has a current active membership of 3000 people and is the mother church of the international movement which consists of over 1000 churches in 31 nations. The church was pioneered in 1974 with 25 people meeting in a living room and has seen tremendous growth primarily through evangelism.

Brian has written leadership training material in the areas of discipleship, mentoring, home cells and identifying individual's giftings and talents and activating them in church life. Many of the Movement's churches throughout Australia and overseas use the material he has written and developed. He has begun conducting training seminars in various cities and towns throughout Australia and overseas. Brian recently preached at two city-wide crusades in Taiwan where over 650 people came to faith in Jesus. During the day he conducted training seminars for pastors and leaders.

Throughout the fifteen years he has been a pastor he has seen many new Christians and older Christians fall away from the faith. This deeply moved his heart to search the Word of God and discover truths to guide people into enduring faith. During the past ten years he has progressively implemented many of the keys incorporated into this book in the church's teaching and training materials. As a result, the church has seen many people grow and mature in their relationship with God. One of the passions of his life is to build Christian lives as a "wise master-builder" and to watch over them with a "godly jealousy" establishing them firmly in Jesus.

Citipointe International
Institute of Ministry

Citipointe International, in Brisbane, Australia is the premier Ministry Training College of the Christian Outreach Centre Movement. The Institute trains full-time, part-time and distance learning students. Programs include:

- Certificate III in Church Community Practice (Counselling)
- Certificate IV in Church Ministry Practice (Youth Ministry, Biblical Studies or Creative Arts)
- Diploma of Ministry*
- Advanced Diploma of Church Leadership
- Bachelor of Ministry*
- Graduate Diploma of Ministry Studies*
  *Note: These courses are awarded by Christian Heritage College, which is accredited by the Queensland Minister of Education and is recognized nationally and internationally under the Australian Qualification Framework.

All inquiries may be directed to The Registrar at:
322 Wecker Road Mansfield Brisbane Australia
PO Box 2111 Mansfield DC QLD 4122 Australia
Phone: +61 (0)7 3343 8888 Fax: +61 (0)7 3343 9291
Email: ciim@coc.org.au
Web: www.ciim.coc.org.au

Citipointe Christian Outreach Centre

Contact Citipointe Christian Outreach Centre at:
322 Wecker Road Mansfield Brisbane Australia
PO Box 2111 Mansfield DC QLD 4122 Australia
Phone: +61 (0)7 3343 8888 Fax: +61 (0)7 3343 9291
Email: mail@cpcoc.org.au
Web: www.cpcoc.org.au